P9-CIW-752

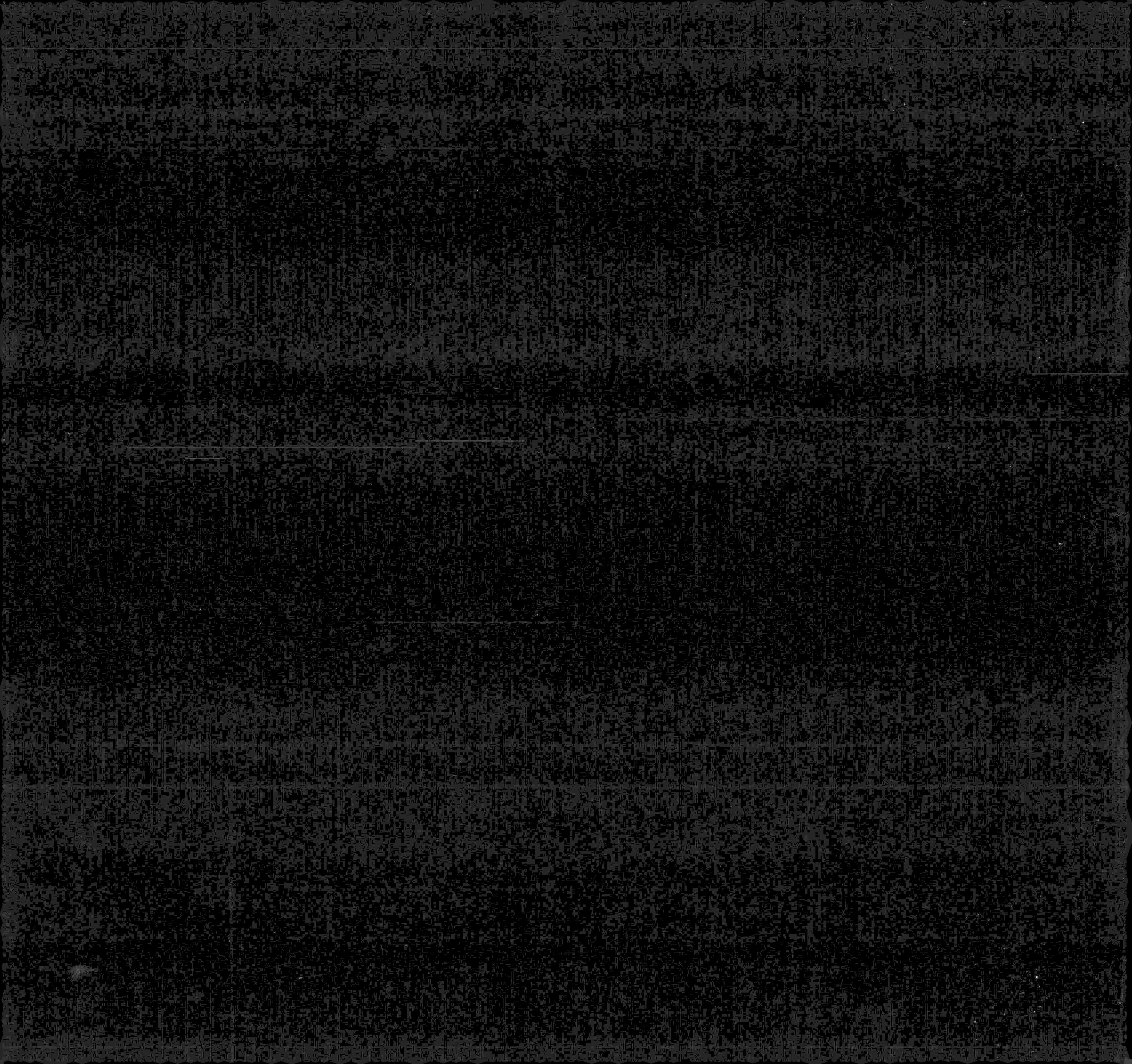

MAJESTIC HORSE

BARNES & NOBLE BOOKS
NEW YORK

The horse has had a deeper and more lasting influence on the history of mankind than any other creature. No other animal has experienced such a close and ongoing partnership with the human being. Continents have been discovered on horseback and empires conquered, the horse has helped to transport goods and develop the culture of travel. Thus it has determined the fate of communities and nations, been decisive in victory or defeat, in wealth and poverty, indeed even in life and death. Domestication of the horse brought about a fundamental change in people's lives. And the change instigated by industrialisation at the end of the 19th century was equally revolutionary. Within just a few decades the horse became virtually redundant, in agriculture just as in the army or as a means of transport for people and goods. The entire species seemed almost threatened by extinction when, just in time, the horse was re-discovered – as an ideal partner for sport and leisure time. Special efforts were made to maintain endangered breeds. Equestrian events, horse shows and holidays on horseback enjoyed a tremendous revival. The number of equestrian centres multiplied within only a few years. The partnership between the human being and the horse was revived – it has since taken on a new quality, but one which is no less intense. Whereas formerly the horse's principal value was as a work animal, now idealistic values are becoming increasingly important. Horses help us to assimilate a hectic, technological society. They have become compensation, a valuable counter-weight for the modern stress we experience in a rational, success-orientated environment. Through the horse we can re-gain access to a world which has become alien to many people as a result of an otherwise functional and abstract way of life.

This happens most easily in the case of horses which are able to live in freedom. Away from the stables and paddocks, a horse reverts to its original wild self – its true beauty, grace, the perfection of its body can only be completely exposed in total freedom. In this state the horse reveals those mythical dimensions which have made it so special throughout the ages, this creature which was born with divine dignity out of the waves of the sea. The universe of the horse, wherever we enter it, is full of fantastic secrets for us to discover. My journeys along the trails of different horses are always full of adventure and delight. In the Argentinean Pampas I felt the earth tremble as a herd of five hundred horses thundered right past me. In the Rocky Mountains the cold wind crept into my bones as I shared the hard life of the real cowboys and their working horses. In the Alps of South Tyrol I discovered my love for Haflingers in icy temperatures at a height of 2000 metres. In India I was able to discover the secret of the Marwari ears and in Lesotho to discover the magic of Africa riding on a Basuto Pony. Way up in the Polar Circle, in the midst of a most dreadful conflict between the elementary forces of nature, I lost my heart to Iceland and the Icelandic Horses.

On all these adventurous journeys I also discovered an important fundamental truth: that the world of horses unites horsey people throughout the whole world quite regardless of different cultures or languages. These animals radiate a universal energy which everyone in the world can understand – if the will and inclination is there. This book is an invitation to join me on my journeys of discovery around the world. It is intended to fascinate and inspire you to keep wanting to make new discoveries about the horse. The individual chapters are not limited to factual descriptions and plain pictures, rather they relate some of my very personal experiences and encounters – in words as well as visual images. The fact that these experiences took place in India, Africa or South America is not so significant. If you go to the next field where horses are grazing, you will be able to feel everything which I am trying to convey in these pictures and texts: the experience of that wonderful power which horses exude; the experience of the inner wealth of deep, genuine, trusting affection which they give us; the experience of a relationship which is so steadfast and strong that it has survived many thousands of years – and will still continue to accompany us into the future.

MAJESTIC HORSE

Gabriele Boiselle

FRIESIAN HORSES

The magnificent black pearls from Friesland
Baroque horses with irresistible charisma

WESTERN HORSES

From the Mustang to the Quarter Horse
Hard-working horses with cow-sense and lots of stamina

HAFLINGERS

Charming palominos from the Alps
From working horses to versatile leisure horses

ARAB HORSES

Horses of breathtaking beauty and grace
Refining influence on all breeds - Darling of all people

BASUTO PONY

Ponies from the kingdom Lesotho
In the heart of Southern Africa

ANDALUSIAN HORSES

Majestic horses with tremendous elegance
Natural abilities required for haut ecole

CRIOLLOS

At home in the wide expanses of the Argentinean Pampas
Reliable and robust working horses of the gauchos

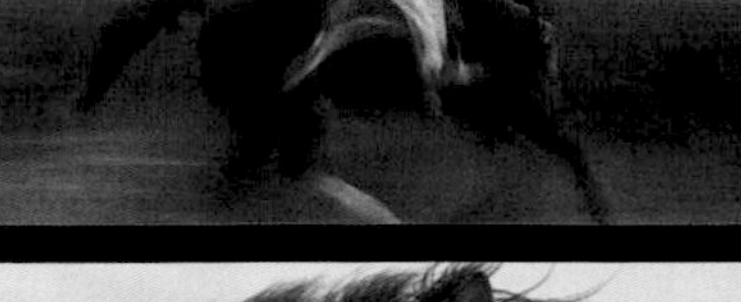

MARWARI HORSES

Proud war horses of the Indian Rajas
One of the oldest horse breeds in the world

ISLANDIC HORSES

Small horses with big hearts
Viking horses from the volcanic island on the Arctic Circle

MAREMMANO

Robust horses from the marshes of Tuscany
Cow horses of the Italian butteri

DRAUGHT HORSES

Gentle Giants with a wonderful character
Renaissance of the loveable heavyweights

GABRIELE BOISELLE

No life without horses

FRIESIAN HORSES

Black pearls from Friesland

It is almost impossible to resist the tremendous charisma of these jet black horses with their flowing manes and dynamic movements. There is something antique about their appearance, they seem like relics of bygone times, and they conquer human hearts by storm.

The sire Jelle 304 with his magnificent neck, luxuriant mane and alert eye is a perfect example of the outstanding beauty of a Friesian horse.

Swathes of thick mist billow in over the dyke and enshroud the horses almost completely. Two magnificent black stallions fidget impatiently in their harness and toss their heads in the air. Their long manes are lashed by the wind. With great vigour a man's wiry hands close up the last silver buckle on the high boots. He presses his top hat down over his forehead, gives a firm pull on the leather of his gloves, picks up the reins and settles himself on the high-wheeled »sjeess«. The stormy wind tugs at his heavy coat and playfully pulls his cape inside-out. The Friesian horses barely even feel the weight of their driver on the vehicle, there is no holding them now, they simply charge off towards the sea. As their hooves thunder over the boards of the wooden bridge two swans take fright, brandishing their powerful wings and screeching loudly. Before the birds' clamouring has died away, however, the pair of black horses and their sinister looking driver will long since have disappeared into the grey mist. After the very last sound of the hooves has died away, a tiny break appears in the overcast, stormy looking sky and a few magical sun rays manage to peep through. For a moment the wild racing pair of horses and their »sjeess« can be perceived as a silhouette on the dyke, the stallions seem almost to be flying as they trot powerfully along. Then they disappear from sight and indeed the whole world seems to go under in the wild, roaring storm.

This is not the introduction to a novel, but rather the description of one of those magic moments I often have the privilege of enjoying during my work as a photographer. To be emotionally roused deep into my inner self, to feel goose pimples stemming from sheer vitality. And to be touched by the wonderful feel of this particular moment, that is what makes life so much worth living. And time and time again it is the horses who give me these moments and unite me with people who share such sensations with me. Two magnificent Friesian stallions lured me onto this dyke. They are half-brothers, *Pandur* and *Rikle*, and they belong to Jelke Wirstra, the sinister looking »sjeess«-driver. He had spent many hours preparing his vehicle, the horses and also himself for photographing and – just as he was ready – this raging storm broke out. He was so furious about everything that he still drove off anyway, right in the middle of the storm. Half an hour later he arrived back, soaking wet, but very happy. After lots and lots of coffee as well as quite a few »Schnaps« we were warm again, the storm had passed over and we started to take photographs – after the horses had been very well dried off.

It is a very special region, this region behind the dykes. The people there, who are constantly aware of the danger of the sea behind the dyke, are taciturn and hard. The broad, flat marsh-land is criss-crossed with canals separating the fields on which the black and white cows graze. In winter these canals are used for skating. White windmills, still functioning today, are a distinctive feature of this landscape, thousands of birds live on the canals, particularly swans – which are also to be seen decorating the gables of farmhouses. Friesland doesn't really have much in common with the rest of Holland. It has its own very old language which, with the very best will in the world, not even other Dutchmen can understand. It has its own ancient farming culture which is expressed as much in the architecture of the farms as in the construction of the very ancient Friesian »sjeess« which, in the original form in which the vehicles are still used today, dates back to the 17th century. The almost chilly, negative attitude to the rest of the world – it could also be described as eccentricity, pride or stubbornness – in the past has created the climate in which the Friesian horse could survive. Without this isolation, the Friesian horse would have long since ceased to exist.

The Friesian farm-horse dates back as far back as the early Roman. It was very robust and tough, and really quite ugly... as the historian Tacitus wrote in the year 100 A.D. During the Spanish occupation from 1568 to 1648 noble Spanish stallions were crossed with the local Friesians resulting in a wonderful horse combining the best characteristics of both breeds. For a long time it was considered the best heavy war horse in Europe. Indeed the Friesian was a very versatile horse with many talents, suitable for driving, riding and also work in the fields. Demand became so great that Friesians were used in breeding throughout Europe. In Oldenburg breeding, as well as in some lines in the State Stud of Marbach clear evidence of Friesian stallions can be traced. And as the inhabitants of Friesland were not only farmers but also fishermen and sailors, the black horses naturally also managed to travel further afield, to Russia and Scandinavia, for example. The Norwegian Dole horse is as obviously a descendant of the Friesian as the English Shire Horse, commonly known as the »Old English Black«. Nevertheless at the beginning of the 20th century the Friesian horses, with their very special trotting action, were threatened by extinction because only very few pure-bred stallions remained. The »Friesch Paardenstamboek«, which was founded in 1879 was able to register 16 pure-bred stallions and 28 mares, by 1913 there were just three pure-bred stallions. Only the committed efforts of some Friesian farmers meant that a pure-bred stock could be assured. Over a period of several decades much work was invested in maintaining the breed. It was possible to see some of these magnificent horses in glittering show presentations at the circus. Then, however, in the late sixties, people began to realise that the »black pearls« were ideal horses for leisure and driving. Since then their triumphal march has been uninterrupted. Today the black Friesian with its powerful neck and magnificent mane is one of the most famous horses in the world. Friesian Festivals even take place in America and no horse show or equestrian exhibition, and in particular no circus, can be held without a presentation of Friesian horses.

Anyone who attends the annual stallion licensing event in Leuwarden in January will meet visitors and breeders from all over the world. They congregate here to give standing ovations to these magnificent horses. There is a very special atmosphere in the hall: old Friesian farmers with grey moustaches stand in their black Friesian national dress and heavy wooden clogs on their feet beside Americans with their cowboy boots and Stetson hats. Both gaze with fascination into the ring and follow the elevated »flying« movements of the stallion who, with his feathered legs and flowing mane, seems barely to be touching the ground at all. The whole hall is alive with enthusiasm, people have tears running down their cheeks, everyone present is in love with these horses – and they are clearly showing it.

Even today the people of Friesland still wear their historic costumes on Sundays and holidays. And the horses also wear their original harness with white reins and white bridles.

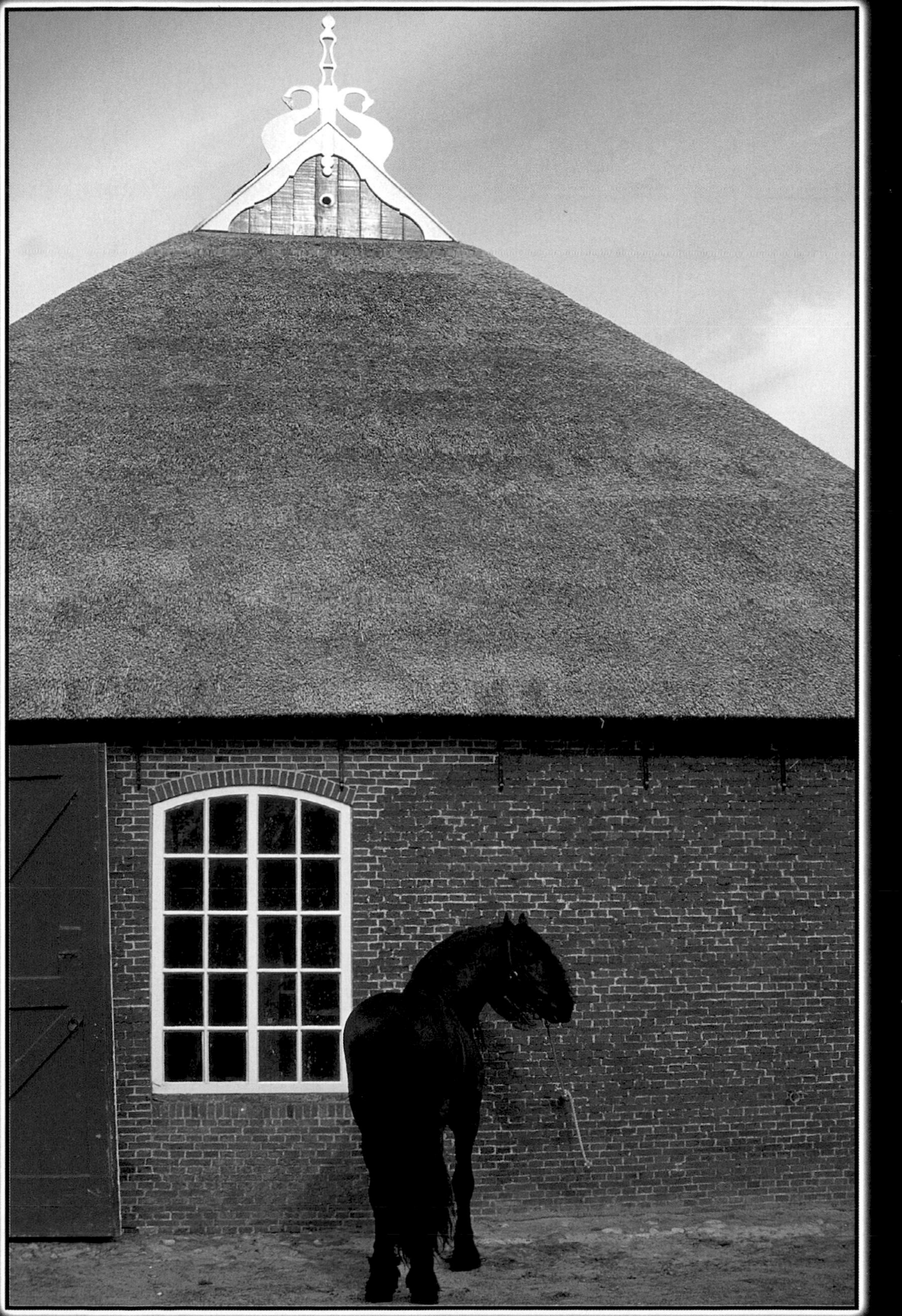

Friesian farms have thatched roofs. The reeds for these grow in the local marshes. The window frames are white, the wooden doors are red - the horses black - all in keeping with tradition. This tradition extends back over several centuries: because Friesians result from the successful pairing of fiery Andalusian stallions and down-to-earth Friesian mares. During the Spanish occupation of the Netherlands (1568 to 1648), a new breed came into being which was to have enormous influence on horse breeding throughout Europe. The well-built and athletic Friesian horses became some of the most sought-after cavalry horses of the time.

From the very moment he breathes, a small Friesian foal is a large horse. His eyes express a sense of curiosity, but also confidence, as he takes his first look at the human being.

The Friesian stallion Marc is an exceptional horse in every respect. With his rider Michael Dannefelser he has a good command of the lessons of the Haute Ecole and he also moves in perfect, elevated style in harness. When his work is done he gallops alone across the summer meadow, enjoying the feeling of utter freedom.

Freedom for a limited time: at this stage the group of two-year-old Friesian colts can still romp about playfully in the paddock. This freedom will soon come to an end, however. The »stallions-in-waiting« then have to do a hard ability test which is held in the Friesian Centre of Drachten and is organised by experienced riders. The Friesians are then presented and evaluated under the saddle and in harness. Only those who achieve a certain number of basic points can even be considered for selection as licensed stallions.

Friesians are good-natured and intelligent and very quick learners. Within a short time they develop a personal relationship and an intensive trust and confidence in »their« person. With this person the Friesian horse can handle any situation, out in the country where he is sure-footed and reliable, in modern dressage in which Friesians are successful up to elementary level, or in harness where a Friesian will draw a vehicle safely through the rush hour traffic or over a marathon course.

The stallion Itz, owned by Günter Fröhlich, has a very striking head and is the prototype of an athletic and harmonious Friesian horse.

The pollen from the rape blossom tickles the little stallion's nostrils and makes him sneeze. In doing so he stretches himself and already shows the first signs of a magnificent Friesian neck.

The stallion Jilles 301 moves gracefully and with such elevated ease. He seems detached from the earth, as if he is flying full of power and elegance - with extreme lifting of the forehand.

WESTERN HORSES

A living myth of the Wild West

Lonely cowboys riding through the wild mountains and deserts of America capture the imagination of all young people. The myth of freedom and adventure nurtures a perpetual yearning for the wide expanses of the American West. Anyone ever lucky enough to ride between the monoliths of Monument Valley along the tracks of John Wayne will never forget the experience.

Denis holds the pencil as if it were a branding iron. His bony fingers, disfigured by gout, clutch the small wooden pencil firmly as he enters the numbers of the branded calves in the worn booklet he always carries around with him in the inside pocket of his rough work jacket. Every now and again he pushes his dented Stetson hat off of his face and wipes the sweat from his forehead. It's very hot again now – although this morning the paddocks were covered by a thin layer of frozen dew. Here in the Rocky Mountains, at a height of 2000 metres, you certainly feel the power of the sun. Nevertheless, there's not much time for a rest because over 100 animals still have to be branded – an almost impossible task to complete before darkness falls. Denis is usually out with the animals by 6 a.m. and he often works for over 15 hours a day. He doesn't count the time too carefully, however, because his ranch is his life. Once the river washed away his house and all his possessions overnight – completely by surprise. In a night shirt, with cowboy boots on his feet, he was just able to carry his two small children on his arms. But he stayed on, and has built everything up again, on higher ground. Denis is tall, gaunt and of an indefinable age with grey hair and a wrinkly, weather-tanned face. He bears no resemblance whatsoever to the romantic image of a cowboy which we have conjured up for ourselves from Western series or advertisements. Real cowboy life is extremely hard and dirty and certainly takes its toll. Thousands of hours in the saddle mean that lots of old cowboys can hardly even walk. After working together with Denis for a few days, I can well understand this. Together with his wife and one son, he runs a small 400 hectare farm in Douglas Wyoming. It's enough to live on, but the family will certainly never become rich here.

Denis from Douglas Wyoming with his wife and the Australian Shephards, his working dogs.

In Denis' veins flows the blood of the early settlers for whom the West was the promised land, somewhere they could live in freedom. Everything which led away from the east coat of America to the west coast of California was wild, strange, new and full of adventure. The horses they needed had to be hard, tough, resilient and have plenty of stamina, not born in stables but out on the extensive prairies. The Mustangs, as we call this indefinable mixture of wild horses, were descended from animals brought by the Spanish conquerors or which had escaped from farms owned by the Spanish crown or been stolen. The horses bred so successfully on the extensive grasslands that in the 19th century there seemed to be an absolutely inexhaustible supply of work horses for the farmer and settler.

The cowboys combined Spanish riding style and English horsemanship in such a way as to develop their own completely individual and distinctive riding style. It had to be functional and practical in order to cope with a lot of work simply and effectively, as for example catching young cows with a lasso for branding, breaking-in wild Mustangs and fighting down bulls – done by means of jumping onto their backs from a horse. Nowadays all these jobs are celebrated as a type of sport: in this way the cult of Western riding has remained much more alive than all the other elements of cowboy culture. Countless films and advertising spots for cigarette bands have made the cowboy into a kind of myth. Anyone, however, who has directly experienced the life of a real cowboy, as Denis, on a ranch, and worked together with him, knows just how big the difference between cliché and reality actually is. At the latest you become aware of this when, after ten hours, you slide out of the saddle, your legs give up completely and the inside of your thighs feel as if they had been rubbed raw in a sand storm. A cowboy wouldn't be anything without his horse. His horse is his partner in good weather and bad. He has to be able to rely on him, to communicate with him without words and to understand him without effort. In addition such a horse must have »cow sense«, the ability to know in which direction a cow is about to jump and how to cut off this way quickly. A good »cow horse« has no colour and no breed, say the old cowboys. There are, however, some kinds of horses which have been specially bred for this work and do it extremely well, e.g. the Quarter Horse. It is the oldest breed and with over five million registered horses, the largest stud-book in the world.

The Quarter Horse (or: »American Quarter Running Horse«) was, in all probability, brought into being in the American state of Virginia as early as the beginning of the 17th century by the owners of the tobacco plantations. Race horses imported from England, the forefathers of today's Thoroughbreds, were crossed with the local Mustang mares which, for their part, were descended from the Andalusian-Barb horses imported by the first Spanish colonists. From this mixture, with such a variety of hereditary factors, a compact, large horse developed which was perfectly able to gallop off from a standstill and could gain enormous speed over a short distance. This encouraged horse-owners to place bets on their horses and to let the animals compete against each other at every opportunity. In these competitions a quarter of a mile transpired to be an ideal distance, which is how the breed were given their name. The races took place along village streets and field tracks, at weekends and on public holidays, anywhere where enough people got together to bet on the horses. Within a very short time the Quarter Horse developed into a perfect »cow-horse«. Speed and sprinting ability on the one hand, agility and balance on the other. Particularly its infallible instinct in dealing with the cattle made the Quarter Horse the best work horse for the ranch. Nowadays, however, big money is earned with Quarter Horses in sport. Descendants of the valuable bloodlines of the big champions such as Joe Bailey and Peter McCue are worth millions of dollars. And »Quarter-Horse-Associations« in many different countries and continents today ensure that, also internationally and particularly for leisure and sport, demand for Western horses continues to increase.

We know them well from the old Western films with John Wayne, the table mountains in Monument Valley, those needle-like rocks around which the vultures circle. However, when you climb the steep sides of the rock ledge with a Quarter Horse yourself, it all looks rather different. Here I gratefully felt how much it means to be able to rely on a fit and well-trained horse. The path up to the Mesa was steep and consisted of stony scree. Our horses, however, knew just where they had to go. Once we had arrived at the top, we had a magnificent view of the bizarre stone towers of Monument Valley. We could recognise where we had ridden over the last days. I sat down in the shadow which my Quarter Horse projected onto the red stones so that I could enjoy at least a little coolness. The perfect peacefulness caught up with us, a lizard jumped around on my dusty boot. I had taken it by surprise. My Quarter rested his head on my shoulder and the hairs on his chin tickled my ear. At this particular moment, I wouldn't have wanted to swap with anyone in the whole world.

Strawberry is how Denis has called his work horse on account of the many strawberry-red markings on his coat. Strawberry was caught as a young Mustang and has been working for Denis for over 20 years.

Monument Valley. It's so still, you almost begin to hear the silence. This is a magical place, a sacred valley of the Indians. On the walls you see rock carvings which are several thousand years old. For many centuries the Navajo Indians have lived here in absolute defiance of the harsh climate and aridness. In the past they survived attacks by the Spanish and white Americans as well as raids launched by other Indian tribes. In 1868 part

of their original country was promised to them as a reserve. This area also included Monument Valley. In 1938 John Ford made his film »Ringo« starring John Wayne in Monument Valley, thus making it famous throughout the world. Since then the scenery has served as an impressive background for numerous advertising spots, films and photographs.

Of all Western horse breeds, the Appaloosa is certainly the most attractive. Breeders of this horse were the Nez Percé Indians. Today there are many crossings with Quarter Horses, however the real Appaloosa should be between 14.2 and 15.2 h.h. and of a tough and strong constitution. The skin around the nostrils and the genital area is often speckled. There are many colour patterns of which only a few are recognised for the Stud Book, for example the spotted horse.

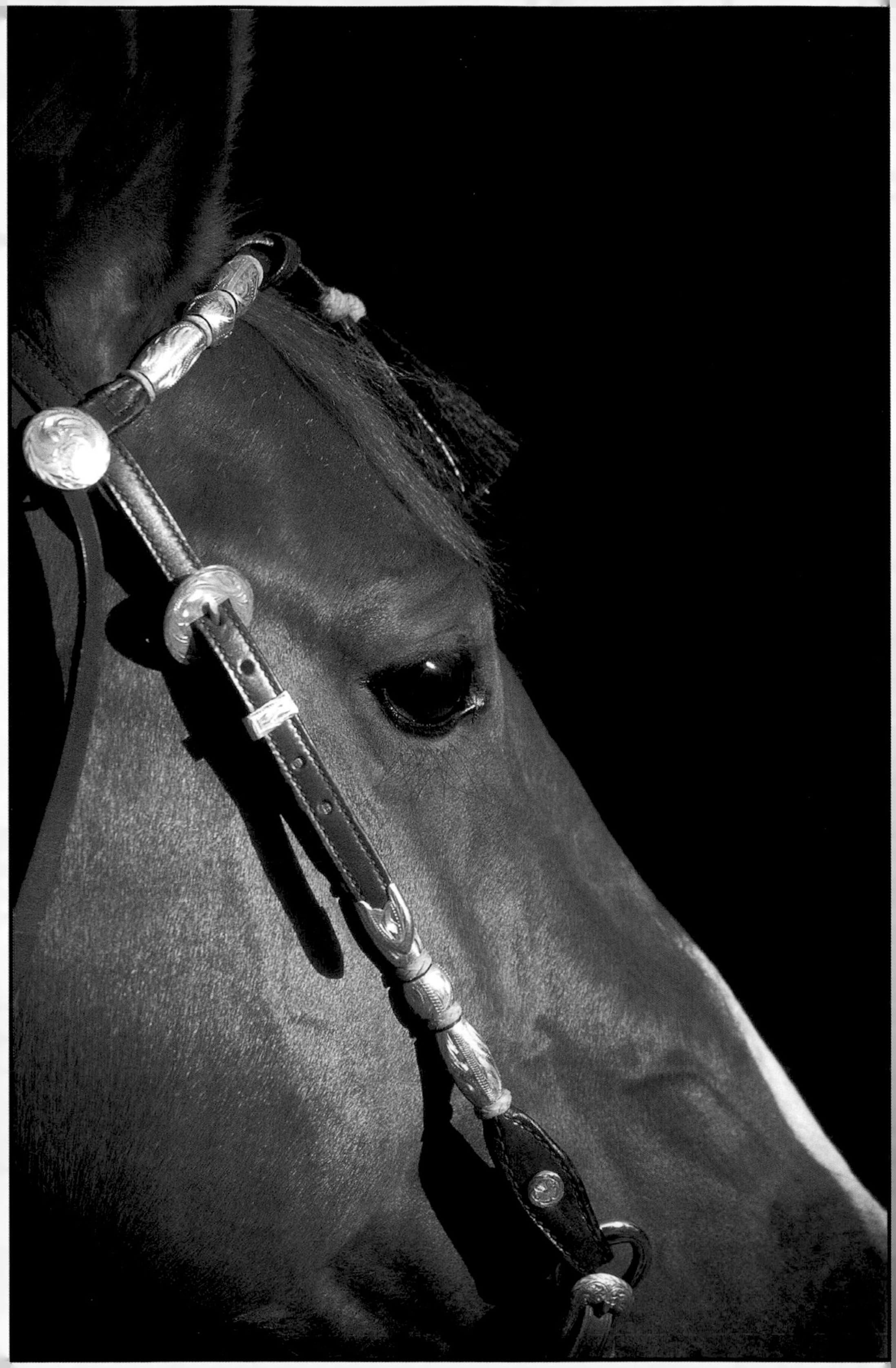

The finely made headpieces are so artistically decorated with silver jewellery and plaited horse hair. Each region and each culture, whether Mexican, Indian or American, has developed its own style which is reflected in different ornaments and decorations.

The Quarter Horse is America's Western horse No. 1. with millions of registered horses. It is the perfect cow horse, bred for work with cattle on the huge ranches of the west. It is a very muscular horse standing at 15.00 to 16.00 h.h. with immense stamina and will to work.

Although you can already recognise the potential for a good muscular system with young Western horses, as this four year-old stallion, it is only with training and increasing age that the compact, athletic expression, so typical for the breed, fully develops.

The Quarter Horse foal frolicking across the meadow already shows the first signs of a good muscular system with its powerful hindquarter movements. He could have a promising future ahead of him. To observe foals is one of the most wonderful things in the world.

Creeping up carefully on an Appaloosa foal enjoying a quiet rest gives you the opportunity of taking such an exceptional photo.

I met up with this older, down-to-earth Appaloosa in an Indian reserve. Next to the shop, the old trading post has a stable where the Indians put there horses whilst shopping. Here they could buy everything for their everyday needs in this shop run by the »white man«. In exchange for such goods they brought their hand-woven carpets or the artistically woven basket work for which some Indian tribes were famous.

SAWYER
MAY-1905

Only Quarter Horses with hard hoofs and strong tendons can cope with the demanding conditions in the mountains and stony deserts. It is precisely this iron constitution, however, which makes the breed the most versatile horse in America. Quarter Horses - and all related crossings - are so widespread in the United States that they are to be found on practically every ranch and in every equestrian centre. Breeding Quarter Horses today is a lucrative business. At auctions high prices are achieved and some very successful sires cost a fortune.

Page 44/45
The Indian summer submerges this valley, which borders on Yellowstone National Park, in wonderful golden colours. Here in the heart of Wyoming is the farm of Bayard and Mel Fox who are often away travelling with their company, which offers equestrian holidays throughout the whole world.

Cheyenne was a wild Mustang mare who had already broken the bones of many cowboys and quite simply refused to let any rider remain on her back. Her fate was already sealed, the next day she was to be taken away, slaughtered and processed into soap. Then she met Peer Vogel, a horse whisperer from Norway who fell in love with her on the spot. With endless patience he managed to approach her and gain her confidence. This alone took up a whole week. Step be step the two came increasingly close together and after a further week she allowed him to put on a saddle and even took his weight. Peer simply couldn't be separated from her. At the John F. Kennedy Airport in New York he walked with her on a rope to the freight plane to Norway. Today Cheyenne climbs through the Norwegian mountains as if they were the Rockys.

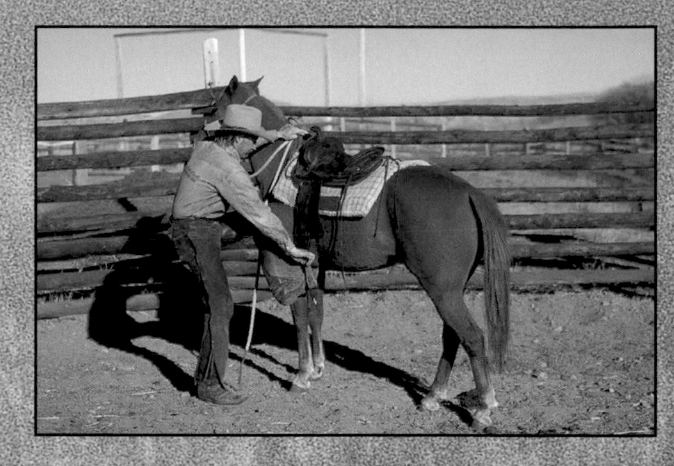

Denis is tall, gaunt, taciturn and pretty stubborn. He has a very infectious laugh and a darned hard life. Two thousand cattle graze on his ranch in Douglas Wyoming. They hardly make him rich but do guarantee a living. This means grinding work in the saddle, often from early in the morning until late at night.

Okie Isma Dad is a truly picturesque Quarter Horse, with a powerful neck, dynamic movements and lots of expression.

»Cutting« is a very special job for the horse as well as for its rider. Only horses which are born with innate cow-sense are suitable for this task of separating (cutting) a cow from the herd, which involves cat-like movements and great athletic prowess. The rider does not give the horse any aids during the work. Within fractions of a second the horse has to know what the cow is going to do so as to maintain the advantage at all times. Cutting horses perform great services for the American cowboys and cutting has meanwhile achieved the status of a sporting discipline. An outstanding expert in this discipline is Jean-Claude Dysli who, 30 years ago, was the first person to import Western horses to Europe.

Nobody ever forgets the view of a herd of a thousand horses approaching in a cloud of dust. The wind carries the whinnying of the horses and, like the beating of a shower of rain, the trampling of hooves becomes increasingly loud. With great skill and equestrian ability, the cowboys master their work which demands incredible energy and application by human being and horse.

Page 54/55
In the barren countryside of the Rocky Mountains the Mustangs look for fresh green and use their hooves to dig out roots they can eat. Only the strongest animals survive the winter and mares do not give birth to their foals until late spring, after the last snow has melted.

In the past »horse drives«, the driving of horses over large distances, were a frequent event. Today, however, it is rare to have really large herds numbering 800 to a thousand horses such as on the Sombrero Ranch in Colorado. The horses, which work on many different ranches during the summer, all return to the mountainous wilderness on 1st December. They remain there for six months without any form of human intervention. They rummage for food beneath the snow and break the ice in the streams in order to get fresh water. Many of the horses are Mustangs which were born into these harsh surroundings. The other horses learn to adapt quickly and to survive. In early summer the horses are all brought together and the long trek back to the ranch with 1000 horses over 100 miles for the summer work begins.

Winter in the Rocky Mountains is extremely harsh. At a temperature of minus 20° centigrade and snow a metre deep, it is very difficult to make progress with horses. Ray Heid takes me with him on a trail through the glittering magical snow landscape of Colorado, which he undertakes with his tamed Mustangs.

HAFLINGERS

Mountain horses and members of the family

The Tyrolean Alps are the homeland of Haflinger horses. They have the sure-footedness of a mountain horse, the charm of an Arab, the riding qualities of a warm-blood and the willingness to work of a draught horse. They have such a pleasant temperament that they make wonderful leisure horses and their proverbial good-nature makes them excellent horses for children and teenagers.

The Haflinger stallion Winterstein from Fohlenhof Ebbs is a wonderful example of this breed.

The stable door makes a dull thud as it closes behind me. The wooden bolt slots back into position and any noise from outside is swallowed up by the utter stillness of the stable, with its wonderful and comforting smell of warm animals and sweet hay. Before my eyes have even become accustomed to the darkness, my ears pick up some familiar stable noises: the gentle rattling of a chain, energetic pulling at a hay bale and powerful munching of straw between the cows' strong jaws. Lots of icicles hang in a row in front of the door. They sparkle in the winter sunlight at a temperature of minus 20°C and sharp frost. Here in the stable it is warm and cosy. And it smells of dairy cows and horses. A few sunrays penetrate through a small stable window, and dance around the small grains of dust in the air. Gradually I can recognise more. The hefty rumps of four cows smile at me. Curiosity overcomes them and they turn their powerful heads towards me and gaze at me with great interest and curiosity because visitors here are a rare occurence. A small calf stands at his mother's side and is obviously pleased about my visit. Its huge eyes peep over a wooden half-wall which closes in his mini-stable. My fingers run through his soft and slightly curly coat as his small, rough tongue licks my cheek. Whilst we are still smooching with each other, I feel a gentle nibbling at my jacket from behind. When I turn around, I see a foal before me. His coat is the same light brown colour as the calf's, but the foal also has light, radiant mane hair, still standing upright. His mother, a magnificent old Haflinger mare has her place in the stable next to the cows and she looks at me attentively with her large, intelligent eyes. My heart leaps with joy at this perfect peace which I have the privilege of enjoying in this old stable.

Here in South Tyrol, near the small village of Haflingen, is the origin of Haflinger breeding. For many centuries small, robust horses have transported goods backwards and forwards along the mule tracks across the Alps between Italy, Austria and Germany. These horses, really descendants of the Noriker horses, which date back as far as early Roman times, were refined and improved in the 19th century by mating them with oriental crossbreeds. In the course of time a new breed came into being which, quite miraculously, combined the best features of two very different types of horses. Just as the forefather, named *Folie 249*, who was born in South Tyrol in 1874, the Haflinger cannot deny his Oriental background. Nowadays Haflingers are one of the most popular equestrian breeds in Europe and there are active breeds societies all over the world. The typical brandmark with the »H« in the middle has become a typical symbol for this race. Haflingers are used for many different purposes: for leisure riding, Western riding, as a driving and sport horse and also, of course, for the traditional sleigh races. Naturally the mechanisation of agriculture did not come to a halt in front of the mountains of south Tyrol, where the Haflingers are at home. However, there are still enough old farms located above the tree line where the land to be worked is so steep that no machines can be used. This is also the case with the Wassner farmer, whose farm is now being run by the third generation. Life here is not easy, it is a very simple and meagre existence, as is reflected in the furnishings of the farmhouse. In the big living room, dominated by the large solid oak dining table and the crucifix in the corner, there is certainly no great luxury - just a television is to be seen in the other corner. They slaughter their animals themselves and generally provide – as far as possible – for themselves, just as the grandmother did in her day. The house is right next door to the stable and everyday life is shared closely with the animals.

The Wassner farmer is a gaunt, silent man. When he comes into the stable, he closes the door quickly behind him to keep the cold, frosty air, which tries to sneak in with him, to a minimum. He wants to harness his Rosi to the sleigh and go up on the mountain. The firewood, which he cut down in the autumn and is now needed for the huge stove which heats the house, has to be brought down. When he sees me grooming the mare, he just sits down on the straw bales, chews his tobacco and watches me. The sensation of having all the time in the world flows through me like a magic current. As if I could just take up time in my hands and feel it and look at it. Up here in the mountains there are different laws. In winter when connections to the outside world break off, the animals and humans become completely inter-dependent, just as was the case in primeval times. And the horse also reverts to its very traditional role which once revolved around ensuring human survival by means of its strength and working ability. The Haflinger was not just used as a pack horse to tread along the mule paths, but also as a work and draught horse. It transported the loads to isolated farmhouses and pulled the sleighs with which chopped wood was brought down from the mountains. Only the horse was able to guarantee access to the valley or to the next farm when everything was snowed up and otherwise cut-off. The Haflinger was and is a member of the family, and the foal (one is born every year) simply accompanies the mother during her work. In this way it learns quickly and playfully about what awaits it in later life. People also have fun with their horses however, particularly in winter when there is little work to be done outside. Traditionally many festivals take place in January. Everyone meets up with their sleighs, and races are held across the frozen lakes and ponds. The horses still need their exercise, particularly in winter and such sporting activities provide a good opportunity to keep them fit and healthy.

I actually came to this isolated South Tyrolean mountain village in order to take photographs of this sleigh race. Now my camera has frozen up and my car is completely covered in snow. I have not the slightest idea when I will be able to leave again. However, instead of restlessness and frustration, I have been overcome by an unusual sense of peace and composure. Such was my state as I came into this stable. Very carefully, I carry on brushing the beautiful tail of this old mare who has been doing her duty loyally at this farm for twenty years now, and in this time has also given birth to eighteen foals. The farmer still has not said a word. He is in no hurry whatsoever. It is not until I put the brush away that he gets up and, still not speaking, stands up and gets the collar harness. As the door opens, a cutting wind rushes into the stable. With the next breath I take, I feel the biting cold painfully penetrating my lungs. But the foal whinnies with pleasure as it runs outside in high spirits and leaps about in the fresh, crisp snow of the previous night. Perhaps it will spend the rest of its life in this mountain world with its own laws and own time scale. Or perhaps one day it will move out into the »big wide world« and, as an attractive representative of an extremely loveable horse breed, flatter its way into human hearts.

When the horses are harnessed to the sleighs in the Alps of South Tyrol, the foal often runs along beside its mother. Playfully it becomes familiar with the tasks with which it will later be entrusted on the mountain farm.

In October the colts' life of perfect freedom comes to an end. During the summer they have roamed the mountain peaks freely and strengthened their muscles and tendons clambering around the rocks. Now they're being brought down to the valley again and have to learn how to cope with a saddle and bridle. The sure-footedness which the horses acquire as a consequence of this tough rearing, is openly acknowledged by the Austrian as well as the German armies. They are trained in Berchtesgarden by the mountain troops as well as in Tyrol as pack animals.

Page 66/67:
The stallion Saphir from Fohlenhoff Ebbs in Austria is a prototype of the Haflinger breed. With a broad chest, a powerful lower body and long, joyful strides he incorporates all the physical merits of a top quality stallion. He also has tremendous charisma. With his noble head and flowing flaxen mane he steals the show from many other horses.

High up on the Alpine pasture at the Spitzsteinhaus in Tyrol the rowdy stallions have plenty of time and opportunity to test their strength. Playfully they learn to defend themselves, to attack and also to cope with a couple of return kicks. This is where they develop the self-confidence required for success in the wider world later on. At the same time it has not lost its talent as a working horse. It is attentive, clever and always more than willing to learn.

With such a solid natural constitution and tremendously strong lungs as a result of being reared in the Alps at a height of over 2000 metres, this marvellous horse can live to an age of 40 years.

If you ever have the opportunity of going up to the young horses on the Alpine meadows, then you should take advantage of this and spend a whole day with them. There is so much to learn about how they behave amongst themselves, what they eat, which herbs or minerals they find where. You get to know the favourite resting places, see how carefully they climb down over the hillside and with what agility they climb over the rocks.

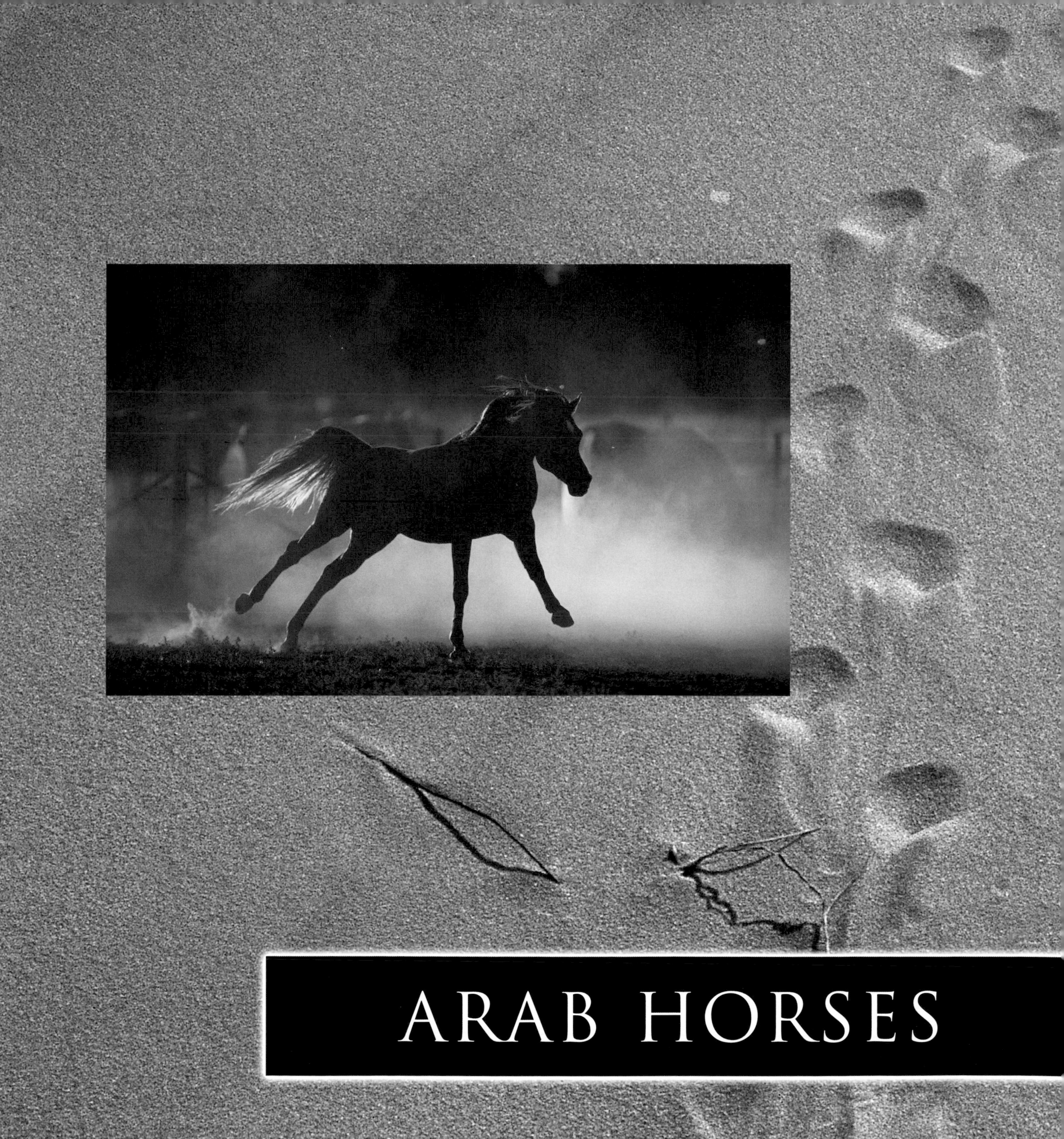
ARAB HORSES

Horses of breath-taking beauty and grace

The pure-bred Arab is a unique breed. For centuries it has inspired the human imagination. Today no other breed is so popular and widely distributed across the whole world as this horse which represents a living unification of beauty, gracefulness, natural noblesse and intelligence.

At the Royal Stud in Amman, Jordan, the breeding of Arab horses also looks back over a long tradition.

The frenetic chaos of Cairo raves around my taxi, donkey carts loaded with mountains of ripe water melons block the routes of jam-packed buses with as many passengers clinging to the outside as there are crammed inside. Small carts full of brightly coloured sweets pass my window. Everything is covered in dust, the houses, the plants, the streets – for months there has been no rain. The Nile is the only source of water for this crawling, sprawling city with over 14 million inhabitants. There will be no more rain again until winter. Unfiltered exhaust fumes from the buses and rusty lorries make the smog over Cairo even more intense. For over two hours now I have been sitting on the sticky plastic back seat of a shabby yellow taxi which threatens to fall apart every time we drive over one of the countless potholes. I have almost given up hope of finding El Zahraa. El Zahraa: the name has meanwhile started to sound like an oasis, a fata morgana where I will never actually arrive. The driver had claimed he knew the Egyptian State Stud, but in fact he had never even heard the name before. My search is becoming a kind of odyssey. Now, in the middle of a high-rise residential area, we are driving towards a long wall. Here I intend to knock for the last time and ask for El Zahraa. When the wrought iron gate opens for the taxi to drive through, an avenue of palms stretches out before us. The large paddocks on either side are surrounded by eucalyptus trees and full of horses. I breathe a sigh of relief, I've reached my destination at last. The taxi stops. I look up and see *Echnaton* for the first time. An impeccable appearance in the shimmering sunlight, ears pointed attentively, every muscle tensed up, he remains motionless for a fraction of a second and penetrates me with his gaze. Then a slight trembling of the flanks, a warning snort with inflated nostrils, and then from a standstill, a great playful leap into the air. Then he disappears, leaving just a cloud of dust behind him. Speechlessly I gaze after him. This glorious grey stallion seems like an apparition from another world

Echnaton became my first photo model, and I spent a very long time studying him. During this time I became more and more at home at El Zahraa and got to know all the other sires and mares. El Zahraa, the Egyptian State Stud, is a stronghold of the best Arab bloodlines. El Zahraa has developed from the private stud of Abbas Pasha, a fanatical horse breeder related to the Egyptian Royal Family, who built a palace specially for his horses on the so-called Rose Island, right in the middle of the Nile. At the beginning of the 1920s the decision was taken to carry on the significant cultural inheritance of the breed which he had developed. With 16 mares and 22 stallions, a large number of which were bought from England, breeding was started again. Initially a farm, Bachtim Stables, was the central breeding place. Soon, however, it was moved to extensive premises near Cairo – which was the beginning of the El Zahraa Stud. Back at the beginning of the twentieth century the stud was already exporting animals all over the world and thus laying the foundations for famous breeds in Poland, Spain, Germany, England and America.

The breeding of pure-bred Arab horses had already been declared a holy affair and made an integral part of Arabian culture and faith many centuries previously by the prophet Mohammed. There are numerous myths and tales relating to the pure bred Arab, more than to any other breed of horse. The exceptional abilities of this magnificent creature and its affectionate attachment to the human being are particularly extolled. The mysterious origin of the Arab breed is another frequent subject. There are many theories here, some of them date right back to Baz, Noah's great grandson. However, regardless of the Arab horse's actual origins, – it has spent thousands of years in the geographically isolated region of the Arabian peninsular where it has developed into a very exceptional breed. In particular the hard conditions of survival in the desert have left their mark on this horse. Its whole life was an ongoing performance test – from the day it was born until the day it died. Under the hardest climatic conditions imaginable, with sparse and irregular nutrition, constant high performance was required. Only a few animals could cope with these kind of demands. Through such relentless selection and the isolation caused by external factors, the pure-bred Arab developed its most appealing characteristics: undemanding nature, stamina, resistance, robustness and speed. In addition to these physical assets, it also has a unique character. Its intelligence and nature have been very much influenced by living in such an intimate relationship with human beings. Horses and human beings were inter-dependent in the desert.

The Bedouins lived from fighting expeditions and plundering raids, therefore they depended on fast horses with plenty of stamina. In general they preferred mares. They were easier to handle and made it easier to continue the bloodline. Many a mare even shared the sleeping area inside the tent, just like a member of the family. Children slept with her and grew up playfully between her legs. Foals, which were often born in the tent, were the best playmates in the world. Only as a result of this intimacy was it possible for the Arab horse's loyalty and devotion towards his master to develop in such a marked way. The legendary willingness to make sacrifices, a recurring theme in thousands of stories, and often so ridiculed by Europeans, is an expression of deep affection between human being and animal. When the nomads were defeated and their realms destroyed, they were also robbed of their horses. In particular the Viceroys of Egypt assured the best animals for themselves and thus founded the breeding of Arab horses as it is known today. The descendants of these desert horses can now be found at El Zahraa Stud. In addition, there is hardly a horse breed in the world which does not have at least some Arab blood in its veins. Following the Islamic invasion in the 7th century A.D., such horses were used to refine almost all European horse breeds.

For a long time it seemed as if the intensive breeding of Arab horses was only being pursued in Western countries, as if people able to surround the Arab horse with the loving atmosphere it deserves could only be found in the USA and Europe. Only a few ruling Arabian families such as the Royal Family of Jordan and the Royal Family of Morocco made efforts to preserve old blood lines in the homeland of the Arab horse. Meanwhile the oil states on the Persian Gulf have altered their attitude towards horses. Some ambitious breeders, such as the Emir of Quatar have bought a selection of the best horses in the world and filled Arab breeding in Arabian countries with new pride. Huge studs in Oman, in Saudi Arabia and the Emirates are not only a wonderful fusion of Arabian and modern culture from an architectural point of view. State-of-the-art technology is used there with regard to surgical possibilities as well as insemination. And so the cycle is complete: because, from the tents of the Sheikhs in the desert, the Arab horse has now returned to the modern palaces of their descendants and taken up its proper place. Once again it is experiencing the admiration and respect it deserves.

Echnaton, the uncrowned king of the Egyptian State Stud El Zahraa, an exceptional stallion with tremendous charisma.

The Egyptian State Stud El Zahraa in Cairo is the strong-hold of the best Arab bloodlines which exist. Horses bred there are of exceptional beauty.

So beautiful, so clever, so sensitive: since time immemorial the human being has enjoyed a very special relationship with the pure-bred Arab horse.

No other breed of horse has such wonderfully expressive eyes as the pure-bred Arab. Mares, as Eyption-bred Kot el Kotoub, for example give birth to foals with the appearance of a filigree creation. No wonder that the Bedouins in the desert cherished their mares and foals as supreme beings and gave them all the attention conceivable. They also strictly observed the unwritten law whereby foals were attributed to the dam's line of descent. Only the mares ensured the continuation of a blood line. For this reason they were never sold. The only way of getting hold of them was to steal them. If this was not successful, you paid with your life. If it was successful then the undertaking was considered a heroic act.

Arab horses are familiar with the merciless heat and the dust of the desert. For centuries they have lived under extreme climatic conditions and thus reinforced their best attributes: an undemanding nature, stamina, resistance, robustness and speed. Nowadays they are at home in almost all countries of the world. They have adapted to many different climatic zones without any serious change in their genetic predisposition.

Page 92/93
Afifa certainly doesn't look as if she is already over 20 years old. Unlike any other breed, Arab horses become even more beautiful as they get older and their attractive facial features even more striking.

The Pyramids of Cairo have already seen the horses of the Pharaohs pass by with their war chariots. And they have also seen numerous kings and other rulers of this realm come and go on their attractive Arab horses - stopping to watch the spectacular sunset over the desert with their own eyes - an experience beyond any comparison.

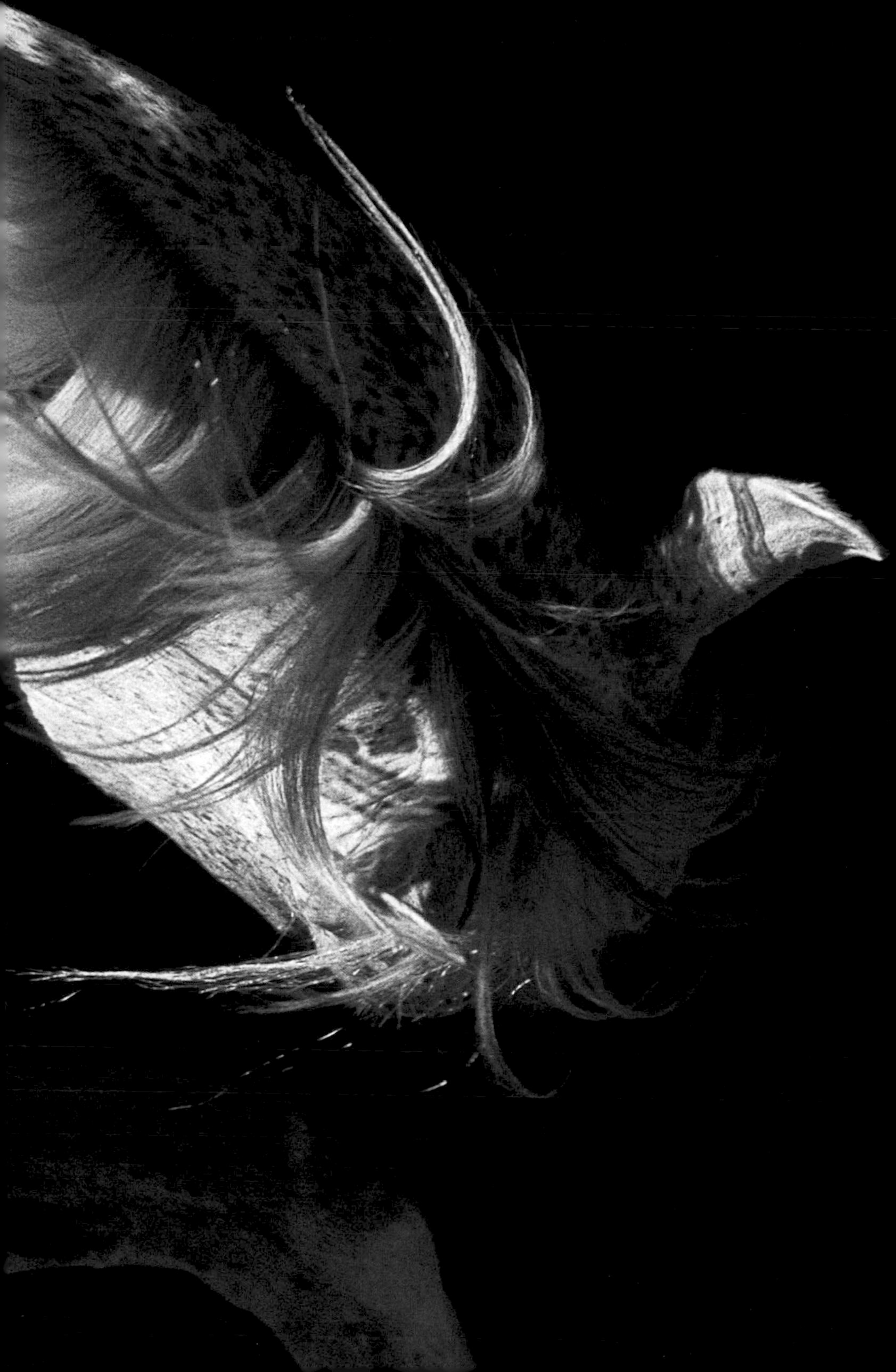

»When God wanted to create the horse, he spoke to the south wind: 'From you I wish to create a being in honour of my saints, in humiliation of my enemies and to the benefit of all who are devoted to me'. The south wind spoke: 'Do that, my Creator'. Thereupon God took a handful of south wind and created the horse. Then he spoke to the horse: 'Your name is Arabian, may the good by bound to the curl on your forehead, the spoils to your back. Your owner I have made into your friend. I have favoured you above all other beasts of burden. I have given you the power to fly without wings, in offensive attack or in retreat. I wish to set men on your back who praise and worship me'.«

(From an Arabian Myth of Creation)

The culture of the Arabian countries and North Africa has indeed endowed them with great architectural works of art made of clay, stone and marble. Even greater than these, however, is the very beautiful living legacy of the Arab horse. In many verses and poems of the wandering minstrels the merits of the horse were praised. In 1064 A.D. the poet Ibn Rashid wrote: »The Arab people express congratulations on three different occasions: on the birth of a son, the visit of a poet in their midst and the birth of a foal«.

The Arab horse always had an almost mystical place in the hearts of the Bedouins. The saying: »Evil spirits never enter a tent in which an Asil horse is standing« is good evidence of this. From these Bedouin tents the horse set out on its triumphal march across the world. It conquered the hearts of all people – regardless of their faith or nationality.

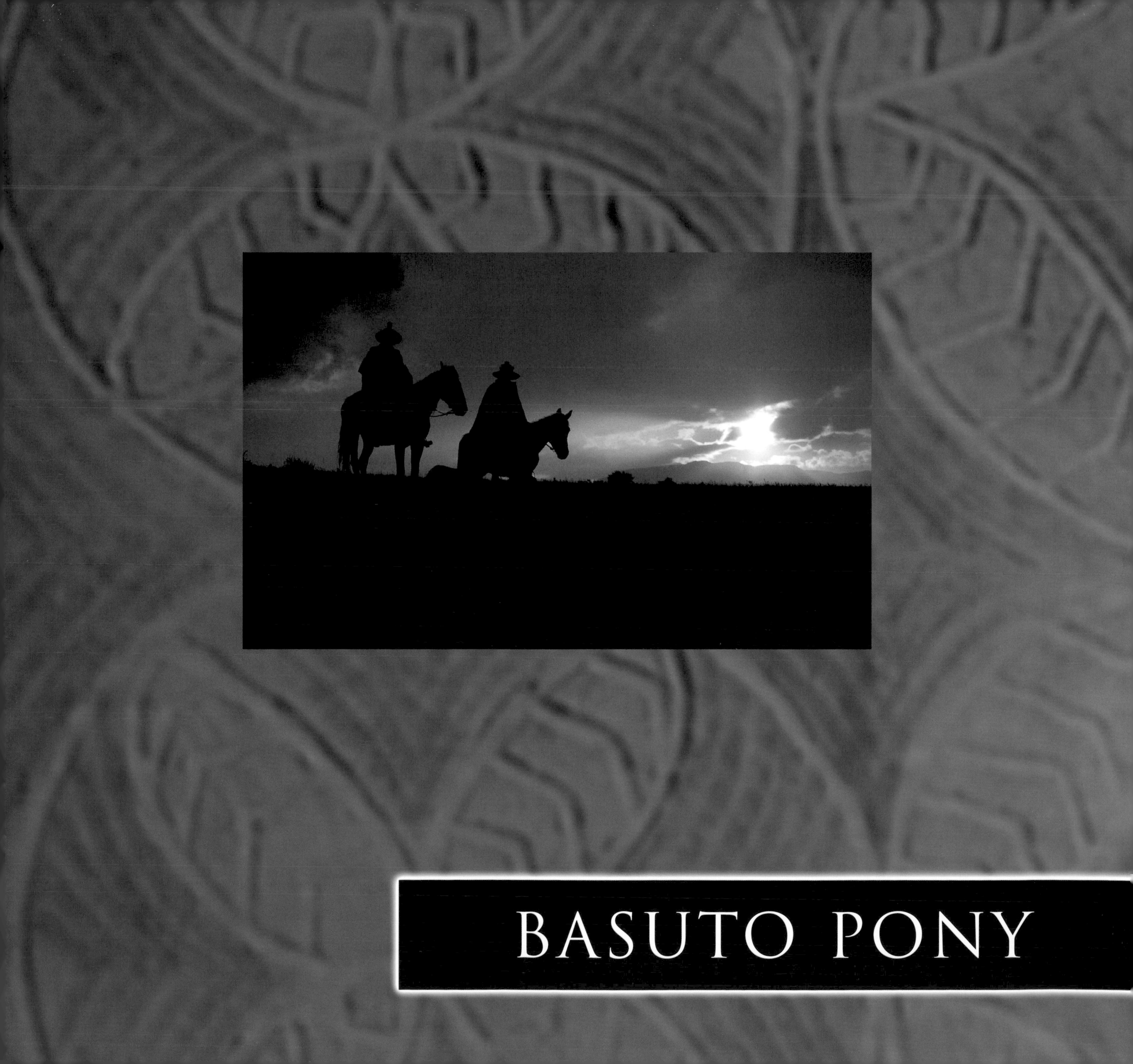
BASUTO PONY

Africa's unpretentious ponies

Here in Lesutho, the kingdom above the clouds, is the home of a very unpretentious, but at the same time extremely impressive horse. The Basuto pony, bred mainly by the Bantu tribe, combines English Thoroughbred, Indonesian pony and Spanish ancestors in its unique pedigree. No other horse is as intensely and variously used in southern Africa as the Basuto pony.

Anyone who undertakes a horseback trek in Lesotho will, with luck, experience a »pink-coloured wonder«, when millions of small blossoms unfold on the mountainsides. Cactus plants with a diameter of up to half a meter are not uncommon.

With extreme caution my little pony mare places her right fore-hoof on the slanting stone slab and tries to find a foothold. She checks again whether the steep gradient of this stone will hold our weight and then, very slowly and carefully, she brings her hind legs up under her body. Silent as a church mouse, I sit in the saddle and barely dare to breathe. I am much too preoccupied to take in the overwhelming mountain scenery. Nevertheless, I somehow manage to perceive threatening black storm clouds accumulating on the horizon behind us and accompanied by very dramatic indications of thunder and lightening. It is still a very long way to the Makhalea River, which we have to reach. Luckily at this point I am still unaware of the fact that heavy rain has made the water at the ford so deep that we will have to swim across the river. At the moment my total powers of concentration are taken up by this very steep mountain path with lots of loose scree and large stony slabs, made smooth and shiny by whistling winds and beating rain. Frequently my finely built mare has to climb across stone pits. She always selects her footholds extremely cautiously. I've experienced so much with this little brown horse over the last days that I trust her profoundly. Just as well actually, because I really have no alternative. The path is much too narrow, slippery and steep even to dream of dismounting.

A few serpentine bends below me, I can see Tseliso, the leader of our little trek, riding along with his red woollen blanket slung around his shoulders, his characteristic straw hat on his head and the bag with feed for the horses hung over his shoulders. A young foal is running beside his mare, leaping about like a chamois on the steep mountainside. Then suddenly the unthinkable happens... a small landslide of stones is set in motion, hitting my mare's foreleg in such a way that all her legs simply go from under her. With constantly increasing speed, we slide together for some metres across a stone slab as if we'd set off from a launching pad. My loyal companion somehow finds her legs again, stiffens herself like a wooden horse and then lowers her head. I remain sitting on her, prepared to face the worst. Keeping my gaze firmly fixed on my mare's ears, I think about the distance we still have to fall. But before we have even reached the end of the stone ramp my mare manages to take a leap, breaking the horrific speed we have gained, and then she does three, four canter strides, bringing us back into balance and then to a halt. When I bend over and look down I see some drops of blood on her hoof – but she continues without conveying the slightest hint of pain.

But then – in the distance – we catch a glimpse of the fires in the small village, promisingly showing us the way, and we hear the dogs barking. As we ride through the cactus hedge into the Kral the children run to meet us, laughing and wanting to help with the horses. The women wrap bright woollen blankets around us, and a big-bosomed black mama comes up to me and – with no inhibitions whatsoever – starts giving my hair a jolly good rub. The goats bleat, the dogs bark and I enjoy a concert of welcome of true celestial quality with its multitude of voices and the sheer joy they all exude. Once the initial excitement has died down the clan chief comes out of his round hut to welcome us. In keeping with the Lesotho tradition, we are then offered a small kalabasse full of home-made beer. It's better not to ask any questions about how it is made, but rather just to enjoy this magnificent feeling if inner warmth – even if you have to cough afterwards. We sit around the fire and eat hot barley porridge with grilled sausages out of a tin. In the flickering light, the shadows of the crackling camp fire leap about like little animals across the geometric patterns painted on the red clay walls of the round huts. Then the lady witch doctor – wearing a crown of porcupine spines and a robe decorated with bright pearls – comes and joins the circle. It's hard to guess how old she might be, especially when she laughs and shows her magnificent white, gleaming teeth. I ask her to take a look at my pony's leg, which by now has become quite swollen. Carrying a torch, we go into the Kral which the horses share with the Merino sheep at night. She takes a few herbs from her embroidered leather bag, pounds them and kneads them together with some of the clay which is also used to build the local huts. She adds water and then some of her spittle to make a really thick paste which she applies to the mare's leg. Then she laughs a shrill and piercing laugh which echoes against the rocks, and disappears again.

The next morning the Kingdom of Lesotho lies at my feet. The highland area, as far as the eye can see, is covered with pink-coloured flowers called »Cosmos« and is bordered by a chain of imposing mountains, the peaks of which are always covered in glittering snow. Lesotho is the only country in the world whose entire national territory is located at a height of over 1000 m. At 3482 m the Thabana Ntlenyana is the highest mountain in southern Africa. The people here lead a very hard life. They only possess the bare essentials for survival. Their Cashmir goats give them very fine wool which provides for a small income. Able-bodied men work in the mines in South Africa and send money back to their families. It's important to be able to afford a donkey or a horse in this country in order to survive. These animals are the only means of transport in a kingdom which has only two large roads.

My little mare, whom I have simply christened »Plucky«, is a Basuto pony and belongs to the most widespread breed of horses in Africa. In the highlands of Lesotho, however, this already very hardy breed had to become even hardier and tougher in order to survive. They rarely exceed a height of 11.00-13.00 hands and have an enormous amount of strength combined with a relatively fine muscular system.

The Basuto breed stems from a cross of the Cape horse with Indonesian ponies. In 1655 horses came for the first time from Europe to the Cape of Good Hope, at that time a base of the East Indian Trading Company which had its headquarters in Holland, and used this as a sort of half-way point on the sea route to India. The first settlers made it their privilege to breed Thoroughbreds and organise races. Hardy Barbs were crossed with Persian Thoroughbreds and descendants of the race horses and, over the centuries, a very strong type of horse developed which was described quite simply as the Cape horse. Arabian and Indian merchant ships, transporting spices and silk from Asia, brought ponies here from Indonesian islands such as Zumba and Java. The Basuto pony is the result of the crossing of the Cape horses and the ponies. The locals very quickly recognised these horses' merits. The small horse integrated into the black culture and later became a symbol of a prince's power and wealth. It happens to be market day when I return to Malealea Lodge, starting point of my ride. There's lots of activity around the trading station. Hundreds of horses are laden with foodstuffs or other goods. You can buy anything here. Di Jones, who runs the Trekking Center, is already waiting for me and greets me with her lovely broad smile... Although her parents were English, Di feels deeply attached to this country. Now I understand why.

This small boy and his donkey are like a telephone line from Malealea. When a horse is required at the trading station he dashes off with his donkey and informs the guide.

The Basuto pony is a successful cross between the Cape Horses, bred by Europeans and also known as Boer Horses – with English and Spanish breeding – and Indonesian ponies from Zumba and Java. The intention behind this crossing was to combine the modest requirements of the ponies with the better constitution of the large horses. Only a short time after their birth, foals accompany their mothers along the stony paths and soon learn how to overcome their fear of precipices. It's a wonder to watch with what agility and caution the youngsters clamber along the paths.

The Basuto pony has a very pleasant temperament although it is no great beauty to look at. It is compact, stands at approximately 12.2 - 13.00 h.h. and is normally brown in colour. Their hooves are indestructible and their tendons and ligaments so tough that a lame horse is rarely seen.

The fortunate breeders were the Basutos, a Bantu tribe who fought against the Zulus around 1870 and were defeated. Together with their horses, they fled into the inaccessible highlands of Lesothos where both humans and horses had to adapt to new and extreme climatic conditions in order to survive.

Since the Trekking Center was established around Malealea Lodge in 1991, the locals have learnt that you can handle horses in a completely different way. A special association has even been founded - it is only possible to become a member if your horse is presented in a well-cared for and well-nourished state. A second establishment was set up by the state in 1983, 30 miles away in Molirno Nthuse, in order to control and maintain the local breed.

This family is particularly proud that their horse has a proper stable. There's lots of snow here in the winter but this horse at least has a dry place to sleep. Normally the horses run around freely in the countryside, thus their fore-hooves are well pared back. At night time they share the kral, surrounded by a clay wall and bordered by thorn bushes, with the Kashmir goats. In every family a young man is given the responsibility of looking after the horses, this is an important function - taken very seriously by this person here. The stallion had been groomed until his coat gleamed and also looked well nourished.

ANDALUSIAN HORSES

Spain's majestic horses - full of elegance and sublimity

Born out of the froth of the sea at high tide - this is how the ancient Greeks imagined the first appearance of the horse. Power and gracefulness united in a majestic equine body, this is the image of a Baroque horse, as it is bred in Spain in the form of the »Pura Raza Espanola«. For many centuries this magnificent horse was an object of prestige for emperors and kings.

The small picturesque town of Ecija is the home of the breeder Miguel Angel Cardenas. His horses with the famous »Cartujano« brand are in great demand - even beyond the borders of Spain.

Just ahead of me to the right I hear a crackling sound in the bushes. Branches break and suddenly a large black bull emerges from the thicket and positions himself on the path before me. »Gabriela, don't move«, says Alvarro quietly. The »Torro« stares at me, snorting and swinging his head – with those huge, powerful horns – backwards and forwards. My horse is an experienced animal, he knows a lot about working with bulls. Alert but calm, he stands face to face with the bull. Then – just as suddenly as he appeared – the bull turns around and disappears again. For Alvarro Domecq such encounters are a daily occurrence, for me it was much more traumatic – and becomes even more so when he tells me that this veteran is one of the bravest fighting bulls in Spain! His courage and performance in the arena were so impressive that he was granted a reprieve and released into freedom for the rest of his life. We ride on over a hill with cork oaks. On the barks of the trees you can recognise the patches where wild boars come to scratch their backs. Then we come into a magnificent valley with high brown grasses, perfectly calm and peaceful in the sun. Two buzzards circle overhead and there is not the slightest trace of cloud in the impeccably blue sky. An intense heat hovers in the valley, there is absolute tranquillity, even the birds are still. On the other side we perceive an entire herd of black cattle, mother cows with their freshly born calves. Caution is required because not even an angry fighting bull is as dangerous as a cow when she sees her calf threatened. This is why we make a detour so as to remain at a distance from the herd. Nevertheless they gaze after us intently and do not lower their horns again until we are out of sight. As we ride through the old town gate of Medina Sidonia, we are immediately greeted by the coolness of the narrow streets and alleys with their whitewashed walls and irregular cobblestones. The clip-clop of the horses' hooves echoes manifoldly from the walls. The cool air between these old walls makes a pleasant contrast to the scorching heat out in the open countryside. This very ancient town was built at the top of a mountain in order to defy any potential attackers. The view from here extends far over the country where the black bulls and white horses are bred. It is not in Jerez de la Frontera, it is here that you can really feel the tough Andalusian heartbeat. Colossal wooden doors with huge iron nails remind us of a belligerent past, about the struggle between Moors and Christians. We ride further up, the alleys become even narrower and the walls higher. Then we cross the plaza with a large fountain where our horses can take a drink. Sticky with sweat and dust, I put my whole face into the water – and see my bull again! This time, however, he is just looking at me from one of the beautiful ceramic tiles which decorate the base of this fountain.

The Spanish horse occupies a particularly prominent place in European history. The conquerors of the new world rode Spanish horses. In the paintings of Velasquez and Goya the horse with the noble head and powerful baroque body dominates the scene. Popes, emperors, kings and other potentates liked to have themselves depicted on graceful, piaffing stallions. And time and time again the flowing, floor-length mane and outstandingly beautiful Spanish eye are emphasised in the painting. The history of horse-breeding in Spain began even before the Moslem invasion in the eighth century. Horses from the Iberian peninsula were already well-known throughout the Mediterranean area in Greek and Roman times. The Roman scribes Plinius and Virgil gave detailed information about the appearance of the Iberian horse. When you look at the marble sculpture of a horse's head in the Roman museum of Merida, you see the Andalusian connection immediately. This means that, together with the Arab, the Spanish horse is one of the oldest cultivated breeds in the world. And without a doubt, the addition of noble Arab blood during the centuries of Moor domination in Spain further improved the breed.

When Elisabeth conquered back the Catholic south of Spain horse breeding with the addition of Arab blood continued. The whole of Europe wanted these horses which were used to further improve local horse breeds. At the time of the Spanish occupation of the Netherlands (1568-1648) the Friesian breed was founded – a breed which clearly inherited its temperament and gaits from the Andalusians. The 17th century was the Golden Age of Andalusian breeding. Royal courts throughout Europe were keen to obtain Andalusians. As horses of splendour and luxury, they were brought to Kladrup in Bohemia, Fredericksborg in Denmark and to Naples in Italy. In hippological history they are subsequently described as Neapolitan horses and as such forefathers of the Lipizzaner breed. New studs and academies with Iberian horses were established throughout Europe, such as the Spanish Riding School in Vienna. With progressive industrialisation and the replacement of horses by machines, breeding in Spain consequently experienced a decline. Only a few families managed to keep running their studs and thus to contribute to the preservation of the breed until today. There, where the very best Spanish olives grow, under the blazing sun on the plateau between Cordoba and Seville, the old traditional studs can still be found today. Since time immemorial they have been linked to the names of important families such as Domecq, Cardenas, Osuna, Escalera, Lovera, Terry etc.

Andalusians are of captivating beauty but in addition they win people's affection by their honest character and their calm and resilient nature. At the numerous annual ferias which are held in every village and town in April and May you see lads riding highly spirited sires through the crowds with the reins, quite relaxed, held in one hand. The feria in Seville and the »Feria del Caballo« in Jerez de la Frontera are the highlights of every year. An important component are the presentations and awards for the best horses. The highest distinction for any horse breeder is to be presented with the golden plate. At the same time in the »Deposito Sementales«, the state stallion depot of Jerez, competitions in »Doma Vaquera« take place, that traditional form of riding which has ensued from the daily work with the cattle herds but has been further developed in Andalusia to achieve stylistic perfection. Hundreds of riders, of all ages and from many different backgrounds, proudly join processions through the narrow passageways between a colourful mass of marquees, with their splendidly turned out horses, wearing silk strips plaited into their manes. On small cushions attached behind the saddle, extremely attractive women sit in their bright flamenco dresses, with the countless lacy flounces of their skirts spread over the horses' quarters. All the big families have their own marquee (casetta) in which they entertain their friends. You stroll through the alleys and meet friends who, year after year, come back again from all over the world – whether from New York or London – to submerge themselves in this unique Andalusian atmosphere. Because the horses, carriages, flamenco and the freely flowing Fino – a dry sherry – all enjoyed under the gleaming sun, make these fieras into an enrapturing experience with a very special »joie de vivre« which is unique to Southern Europe.

For centuries Spanish horses have been indispensable partners for the »vaqueros« (Spanish cowboys) in their daily work in the fields.

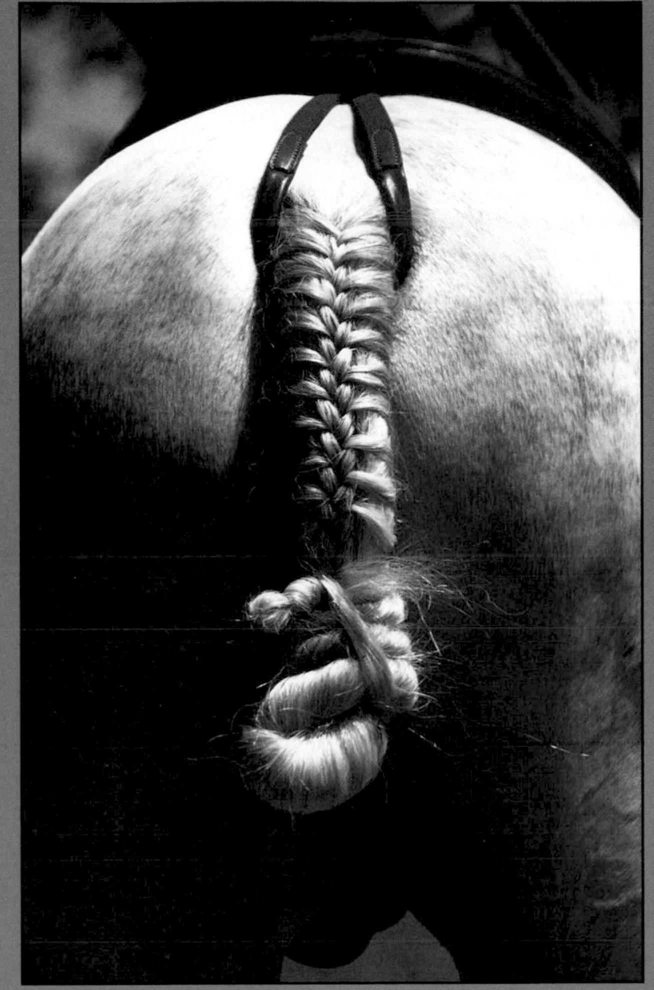

The many different details of bridling up and preparing a horse, including the artistic plaiting and binding of the tail, which may be knotted only, require extensive expert knowledge and practice.

The Spanish horse is more firmly established than any other in European historiography. Courtly pomp and ceremony of incredible dimensions developed around the horse and horse breeding was attributed official status. At royal equestrian centres, such as here at the Spanish Royal Summer Residence in Aranjuez, the great art of equestrianism in connection with court life was celebrated to the full.

A large eye and lively temperament: deep set under huge eyebrows, encased by thick, long lashes, alert and yet exuding a calm, dark clarity, such is the unmistakable eye of a true Spanish horse.

The stallions of Las Lumbreras Stud, which has been in the possession of the Delgado family since 1802, are famous for their Baroque beauty, their temperament and their very expressive pleasure in movement. Its movements are unique and unmistakable, such as this stallion here in an elevated collected canter with flowing mane and powerfully arched neck. The secret of this breed lies in the connection between a well-balanced nature on the one hand and a fiery temperament on the other.

You get to know Andalusia and its traditions best where people are celebrating. And there are always reasons to celebrate. Every guest who experiences one of these festivals will find himself in a state of ecstatic intoxication on account of the beauty and colours, of the music and dancing, also of course on account of the sherry which originates from Jerez and always flows freely on such occasions. For the locals it is a kind of festive lubricant whilst many visitors find themselves completely thrown by its effect. The most attractive Andalusian festivals are the »ferias«, originally horse fairs principally for the purpose of commercial dealings, nowadays a spectacular and grandiose event, a show place running according to its own laws, a setting where the melodramatic heartbeat of the landscape and its people can be clearly felt – and where the horses are the real protagonists.

One of the most atmospheric »ferias« far and wide – an absolute must for every horse lover – is the Feria del Caballo in Jerez de la Frontera, which takes place every May. Every well-respected family has its set place where it erects a »casita« every year, an elegant festive marquee as a meeting point for family, friends and guests. Large clans even possess houses which stand empty for the rest of the year and are only used for the »feria«. To see and be seen – that is the motto here. The men are dressed in the classical riding wear of the »caballeros« – white frilly shirts with short jackets and close-fitting trousers, set off by a flat, wide-brimmed hat. The proud Andalusian woman present themselves in their colourful dresses with the typical flouncy skirts. Only a good sense of balance and a firm grip around the rider's waist prevents them from falling.

Each »feria« is a festival of colours and a kaleidoscope of countless affectionately composed details which together comprise such a fascinating whole. There is a tradition behind every detail - it tells its own story as well as the story of a greater passion, an ongoing passion with which the people in Andalusia have dedicated themselves to preserving their own very special inheritance. Before the »feria« takes place, the coachmen get out their »espolainas« which are artistically decorated and originally intended to protect trousers and shoes. The horses' bridles are covered in hundreds of small coloured bobbles, called »borlas«. Bright woollen or silk bands are plaited into the manes and the tails of the animals. The vaquero riders wear their small embroidered waistcoats, the coachmen their black hats called »catite«. And, wherever possible, the family coat of arms is visible - either painted on the carriage or embroidered on the upholstery. Presentation is very important at a »feria«, although in fact this seeing and being seen is something common to festivals all over the world.

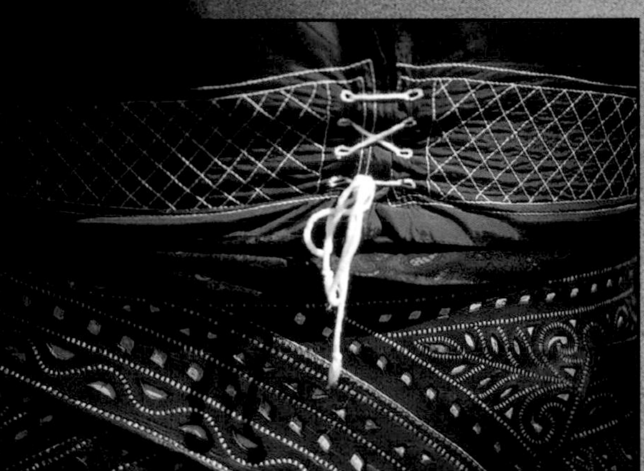
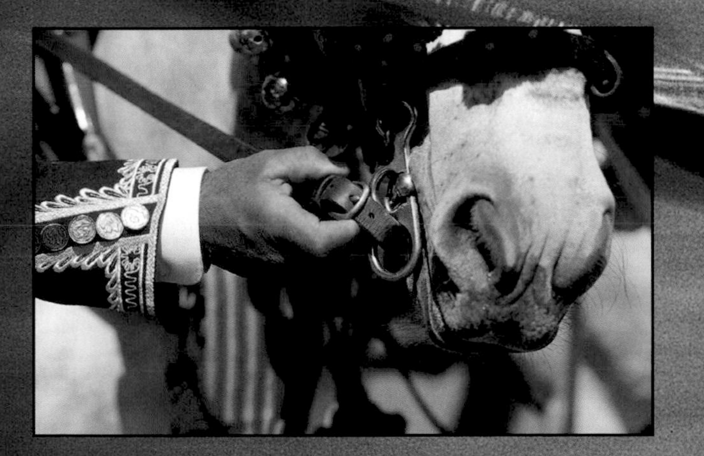

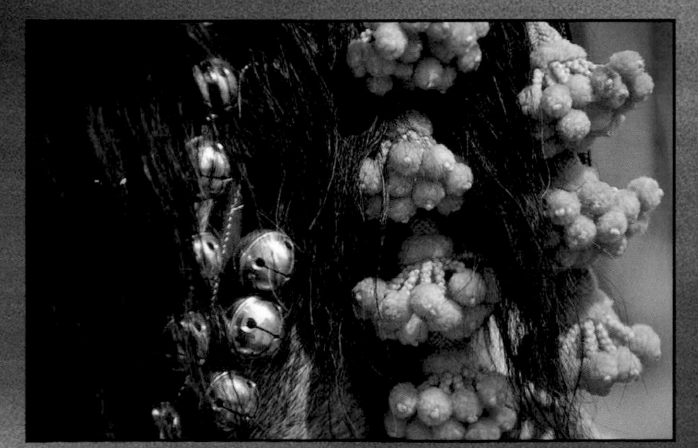

Many of the brown lines which exist in modern breeding today can be traced back to the Escalera Stud in Fuente de Andalucia. The stud has been existence for over two hundred years. One of the few female breeders in Spain, Señora Maria Fernanda Escalera de Escalera pays particular attention to correct conformation and ground-covering forwards movement of the horses. Her »Doctora« line of mares is well-known throughout Spain. Her horses are increasingly being used not only in classical dressage of the haute école but also in modern dressage sport.

In addition to horses, the Guardiola family also breeds fighting bulls. The Andalusian horses bred here have a special instinct in their dealings with the black »toros« because they grow up together with them on the extensive estate. Each stallion is trained in the traditional »vaquero« riding style and stands out particularly as a result of its athletic muscle system and willingness under the rider.

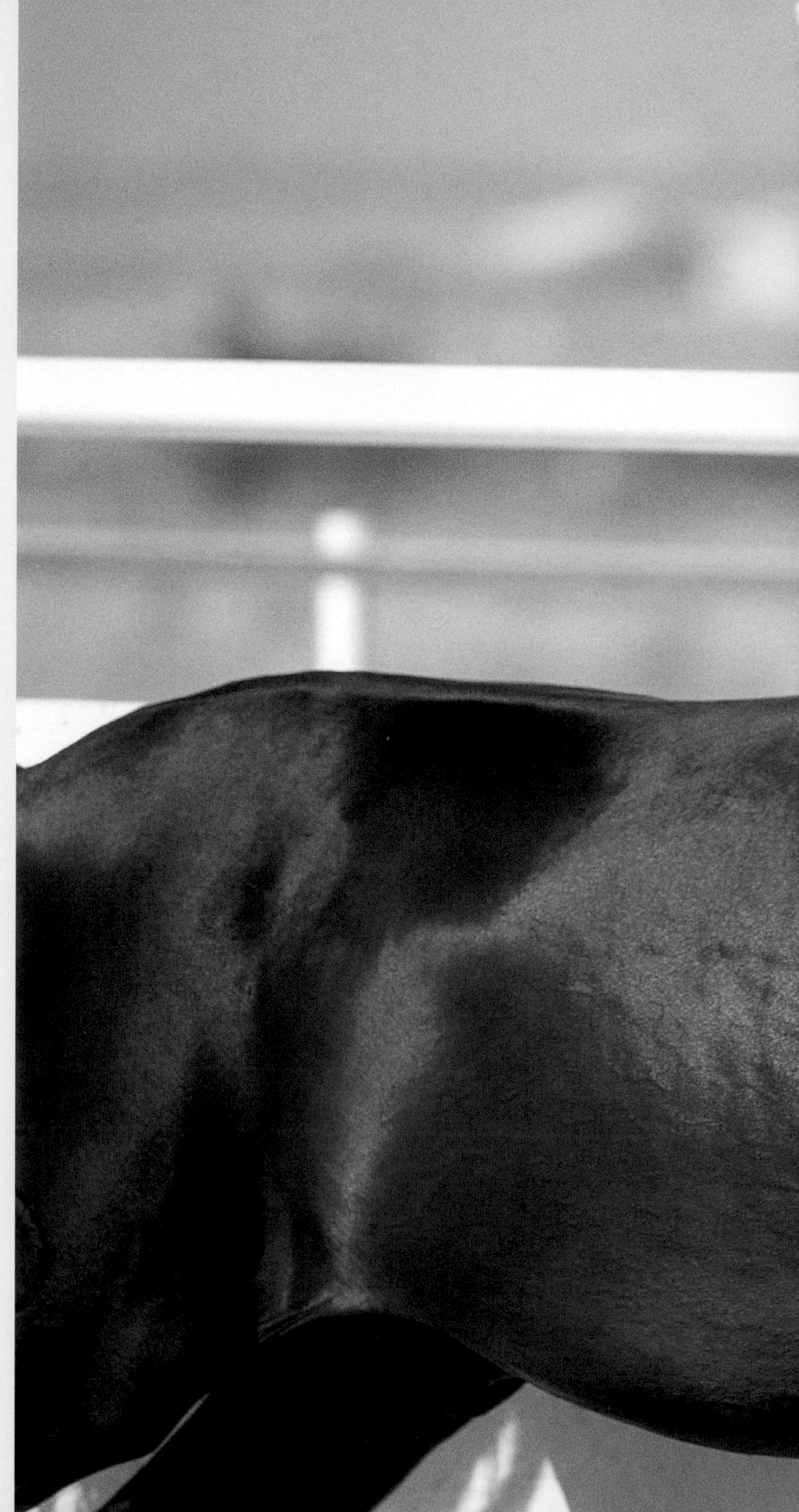

The young stallions at the Lovera stud near Ecija have a wonderful life in a large herd of their own kind. They frolic about and test their strength with stallions of their own age.

The coat, which was dark at birth, very gradually lightens. Even the four year-old stallion Lovera, who boisterously lets off his high spirits, is just gradually getting his light colour.

The mane will also change colour. Andalusian horses do not normally become snow white until the age of eight to ten years.

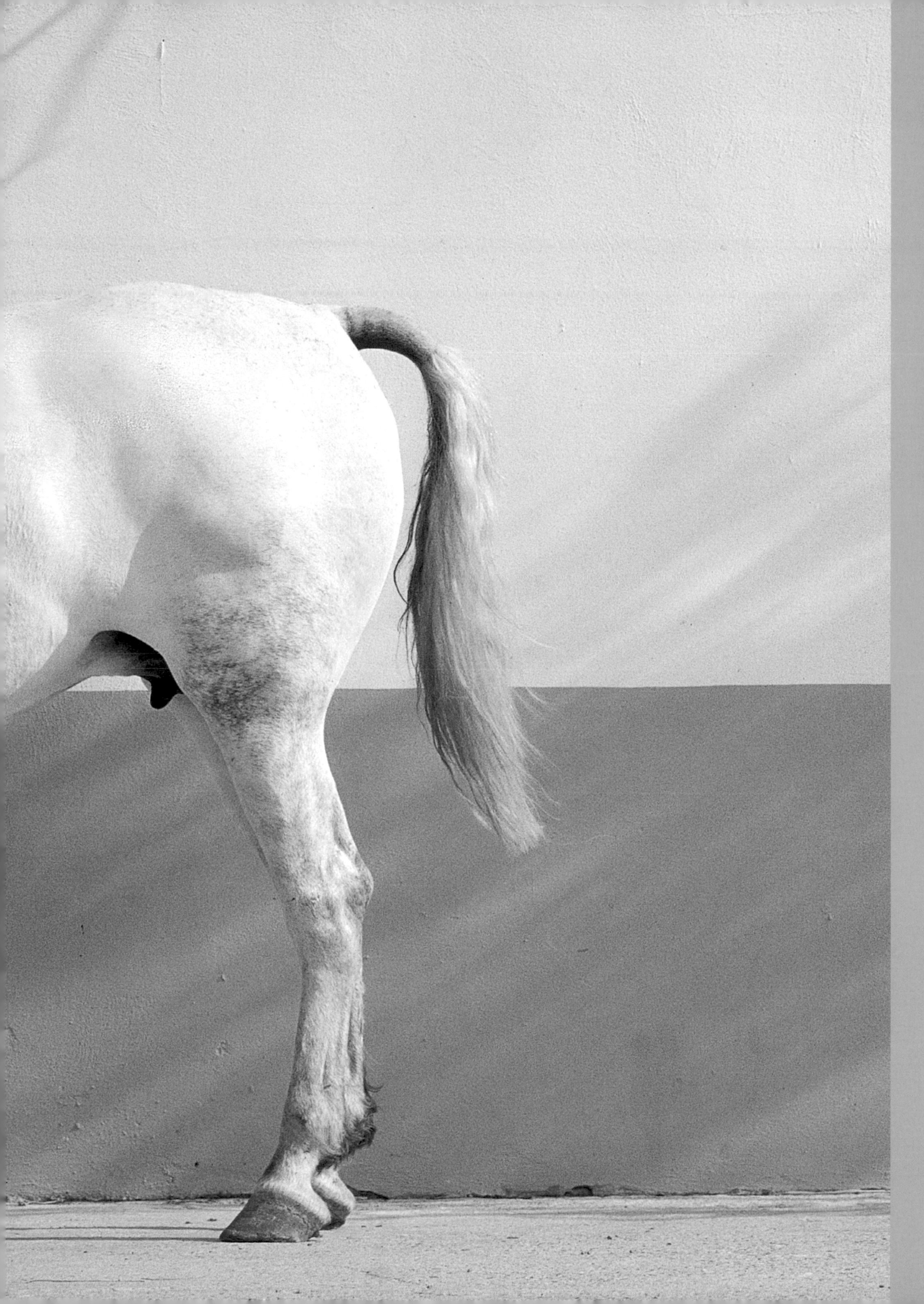

Foals are normally born in springtime, before it gets too hot, and they remain with the mares until autumn. They spend the next years, often together with the black cattle, on the huge estates, in cork oak woods or in a sea of poppies. The young fillies then see a brush for the first time when they are being prepared for the great »Campionato«, which takes place in Seville every November. Then the dock of the tail is shaved and the mane is cut back to a crest following the curve of the neck. This is an old tradition which is still observed, although the mares would get just as magnificent manes as the stallions if they were given the appropriate care.

Miguel Angel Cardenas' stud is famous for its excellent stallions such as »Valido« and »Torbellino«, who as quite outstanding sires have had considerable influence on Spanish breeding in recent decades. The elegant bearing, the high stepping action, the expressive eyes are clear indications of why Andalusian Horses were in greater demand than jewels and diamonds at the royal courts of Europe.

In former times mares and foals remained outside the whole year round. They were just as exposed to the burning heat in summer as the cold rain in winter. These conditions created a hardiness and resistance from which the breed still benefits today.

Mares are rarely ridden. At breeding shows they are presented individually in hand or in a group. In such a case they are only connected together by a neck strap, as this impressive batch of five mares from the Cardenas Stud in Ecija demonstrates. Up to 20 horses can be connected in this way, and then they can be easily commanded to circle around one person.

Under Haute Ecole we understand classical equestrianism in its highest degree of perfection as is practised today at the Riding Schools in Jerez de la Frontera, the Spanish Riding School in Vienna, the Cadre Noir in Saumur and the Portuguese Riding School. Their lessons often relate back to requirements dictated by military riding. Capriole, courbette, pirouette and levade are figures which were frequently represented in old engravings and paintings. Spanish horses in particular were consciously bred for the lessons of classical equestrianism and today still embody the ideal of the Baroque horse. The capriole shown here is one of the most difficult lessons in classical equestrianism. It can only be done by horses with well-trained hindquarter muscles.

Andalusia is different. Anyone who travels to the south of Spain experiences a country of extremes on which century-old conflicts have clearly left their mark. It is a countryside of strong emotions and passions, a magical countryside which fascinates and also poses a great challenge. This is where an exceptional horse came into being, a horse which is unique in this world.

CRIOLLOS

Semi-wild horses working with the gauchos

They are just as at home in the endless expanse of the Argentinean Pampas, in this undulating green ocean of grass, as in the sparsely vegetated stony deserts of the Tiera del Fuogo and the mountain ranges of the Andes.

The work of the Argentinean gauchos is hard and requires unlimited physical application in dealing with the horses and cattle.

The wind is singing in the pampas, whistling through the grasses and snatching the words straight from your mouth almost before they're properly formulated. There's not even a chance of them reaching your own ear. That's why you can't hear them coming – you can only sense it. Under the tips of your boots the earth starts to tremble slightly. Then the vibrations extend over the whole sole. And your eyes turn towards the horizon, searchingly. What's happening? Then a cloud of dust, nothing more, over this sea of grass. And it all happens so quickly. An incredibly fast thundering noise accompanies the vibrations. The dust cloud breaks up, silhouettes emerge, a wall of bodies with horses' heads dancing up and down and flying manes. Suddenly I find myself inside this cloud of dust and thunder. Some horses shy away, break off to the left and the right, the herd splits in front of me and, in a few short seconds of shock, they have me surrounded.

Was I just a little too daring, a little too confident in my conviction about the animals' instincts – that they would never trample a human being? But there's no time left to think. My camera is directed straight into this thundering mass of horses, I simply press the release and shoot. Before I can even grab the second camera, these weird and wonderful apparitions are away, the whole herd has passed. I turn around and see them disappearing at high speed into this green ocean of eternity from whence they came. And last of all, the gauchos come past with their shouts echoing behind the herd. A few jokes are made in my direction – about whether the herd of 500 horses was big enough for the »gringa«. Up to the very last moment they had doubted that I really would stand my ground. Now I remain there alone, the dust billows out of my ears, I can see virtually nothing - and my camera also requires thorough cleaning.

The Criollo breed, as we know them today, stem from the wild horses which had become natives of the extensive Argentinean grassland, the pampas. They are descendants of those animals which the Spanish conquerors and settlers brought with them on their ships from Europe to South America. The stock was founded in 1536 by Pedro de Mendoza, the founder of Buenos Aires who, according to historical documents, brought one hundred Spanish horses to Argentina. Five years later, when the town was destroyed by the Indians, many horses were able to flee into the pampas, where they bred fast and learnt to cope with the climatic circumstances. The name of the breed varies from country to country: Criollo in Argentina, Crioulo in Brazil, Costeno or Morochuco in Peru, Corralero in Chile und Llanero in Venezuela. The genetic pool of these animals is extremely diverse and extends from the baroque Andalusian horse via Berber and Arabian ancestors to powerful working horses with a significant amount of Franconian cold blood and to Galician mountain ponies. Thanks to modern gene technology it has been possible to trace a link to the Sorraia horse – the original ancient Spanish horse. From this mixture of breeds it was only the strongest and most resistant horses which survived, those which – in addition to their strength – also had an infallible instinct for all dangers. They established the basic type of the Criollo with all its merits, just as it is to be found in Argentina today. At the end of the 19th century the importing of European and North American stallions caused a degeneration of the breed. Rigorous selection made by a few interested breeders led to the preservation of the breed and registration in the Argentinean stud book in 1918. This natural and sometimes dreadfully cruel selection meant that an extremely robust horse came into being, a horse which is virtually impossible to match in terms of toughness. It copes well with the most extreme stresses and strains and can survive with minimal rations of nutrition and water. This was quite uniquely demonstrated by two Criollos who covered a distance of 16,090 kilometres within two and a half years. In 1925 Professor Aimé-Felix Tschiffely rode from Buenos Aires to Washington DC with his horses Mancha and Gato, 15 and 16 years old, in order to make Criollos better known in America. The two horses, who had attracted an enormous amount of attention during the trip, returned home together and lived to a very old age, Gato became 36 and Mancha 40 years of age. Stamina competitions are very popular amongst Criollo breeders. In these competitions horses have to complete distances of 750 km in 14 days. This combination of toughness and tremendous resilience against external influences is something it is important to maintain in the breed without, however, over-taming the natural wildness of the Criollos and domesticating their instinct too much. The Criollo is a hard-working horse which, after his work has been done, is released back into freedom and to his herd.

I have rarely ridden a horse as sure-footed and fearless as a Criollo. And, since a particular experience some years ago which has had a lasting impression on me, I would always have blind faith in such a horse: as every year, the foals were being inspected and branded with the breeding mark. For this purpose the horses had to be captured with a lasso and then held down. The work was tiresome, it involved lots of bruises and a considerable amount of mockery for the gaucho who let one of the foals go. The work went on for longer than had been planned, but that same evening, the herd had to be driven into the Corral of the Estancia. As two gauchos had been injured in the branding process, I was asked to help bring the herd back home. For the first time in my life, I swung myself into a »recado« gaucho saddle. I was fully occupied trying to keep up and get used to the flat gallop of my Criollo horse. All went well as far as the river and then, completely suddenly, night fell and the only sign of light was a fine crescent moon which appeared on the horizon. Suddenly it became so dark that it was hardly possible even to see my horse's ears. My original feelings of fear subsided into a kind of fatalistic composure. I held the reins virtually as a simple adornment in my hands. Occasionally the rough voice of Miguel rang through the darkness – he was calling out some kind of encouragement to me in Spanish, which I didn't understand. I could hardly see anything but I could feel my horse's heartbeat against my leg, the warmth of his body encompassed my body and the smell of his sweat mingled in my nose with the dust which the herd was whirling up. We glided along as if we were in a black ocean, pushing a wave of undulating bodies ahead of us. After half an eternity the lights of the Estancia appeared in the distance. To me they were like the gleam of a lighthouse must seem to someone who has been shipwrecked. A gate opened with a squeak. Loud cries, whistles and the cracking of the long leather whips brought the herd to a halt in no time at all. As the gate closed, I slid out of the saddle and found that my trembling legs could barely hold me. Miguel gave me a friendly slap on the shoulder. I didn't come properly to my senses until I was in the pale light of the stable lantern. Someone passed me a glass of red wine, and another, and another... That night I slept like a log and asked myself the next morning as I woke up if perhaps the whole thing had just been a film.

Criollos are one of the hardiest and most resistant breeds in the world. Their wonderful eyes tell of their lost freedom.

In Argentinia are cattle stocks consisting of 55 million cows which are looked after by approximately 150,000 gauchos. These men do the same work today as their grandfathers did before them – just the modern gauchos can use some technical appliances to make some aspects of their work easier. Nevertheless, the catching and branding of cattle, the de-horning and castrating is still as hard work as it was one hundred years ago. Gauchos are national heroes in Argentina, fighters for freedom. They are the knights of the Pampas who help anyone being persecuted and who themselves were subjected to prejudice for long enough. They are singers and poets at the campfire on a cold night. They are the best friends you can have and a relentless enemy if you injure their pride. The code of honour of the gauchos is the moral backbone of a whole nation.

The gauchos wear ancient ponchos which normally are only to be seen in museums. The silver parts of the bridle and spurs are also historic items which were collected from all over the country in order to make authentic material available for the »Escuela del arte equestre« to use in their presentations.

On the long winter evenings the gauchos make their own clothing and tools. Typical headcollars are made from dried gut, sinew and leather. Sometimes they are decorated with silver pearls. Bridles are made from plaited horse hair and from skin stripped from the hind legs they make the toughest boots which ever existed. The entire saddle is based on a »tree« made out of cattle hip bones. It is hand-made by the gauchos and decorated and finished with a top layer of thick sheepskin known as »cojinillo«. For the knife a blade has to be bought, the handle they make themselves from wood or horn. This knife, often richly decorated and called »facon«, is the most important tool a gaucho has. He never wants to be separated from his knife – any more than from his horse for that matter. Also the attractive wide belts are home-made. In former times a gaucho put his whole fortune in the form of coins onto his belt. In this way everyone knew how rich or poor the gaucho was and how much he was able to gamble away in the »pulperia« of the pub. In order to safeguard the belt from getting into the wrong hands it was even decorated with the gaucho's name – appliquéd in silver letters. In the different provinces of the country different forms of stirrup irons are used. They vary between simple box stirrups and wooden discs covered with leather, in which the boot was positioned.

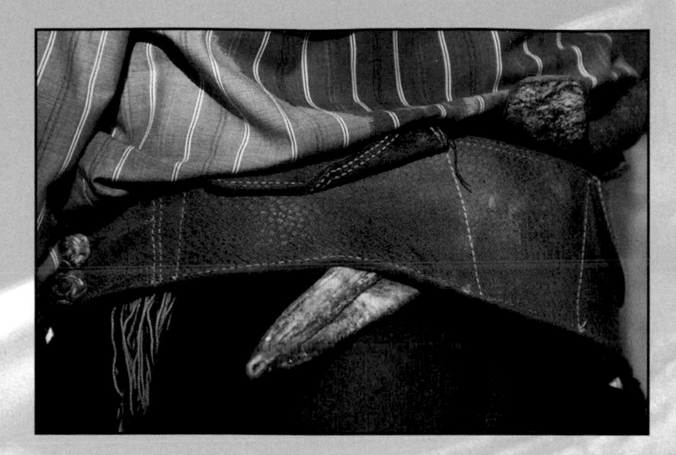

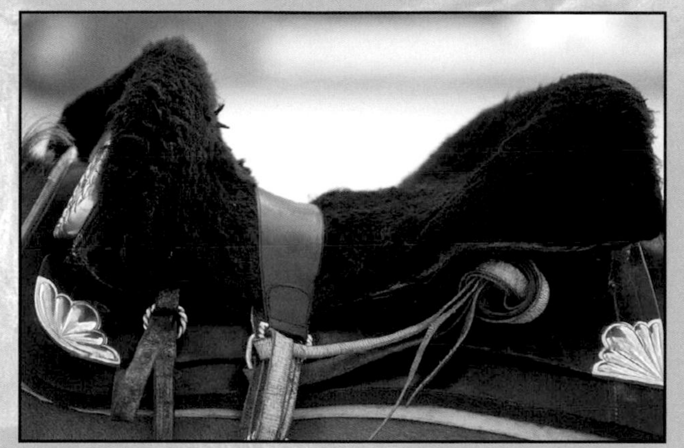

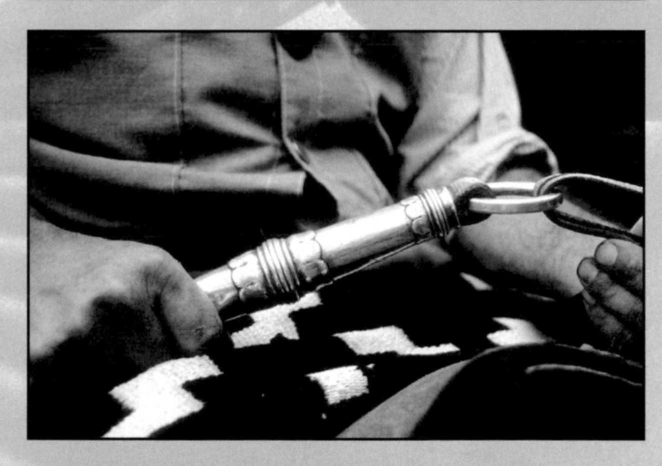

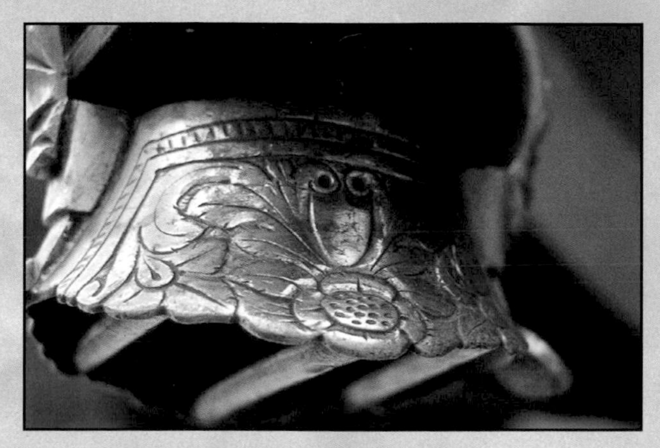

The Domador was a highly respected man at any stud. He risked his bones breaking in young horses. He often had Indian blood in his veins and the special feeling for horses which today we associate with »horse whisperers«. There were different ways of breaking in horses. In the treeless Pampas a trunk was organised and dug into the earth, the palenque. The animals could be tied to this in order to saddle up... if the horses allowed this. Often young horses were tied together with experienced horses. Then they learned - at exactly the same time, so to speak - all the lessons of obedience.

The gauchos love the boisterousness and wildness of the stallion because, just like a captured stallion in a corral, they also long for their freedom and always feel their best riding across the wide open areas. If there is occasionally a dispute between two stallions who are defending their herd of mares, then the gauchos make no attempt to interrupt, indeed they even shout encouragement to the stallions. The winner then gets the entire herd and the loser is castrated.

The gauchos use the surprise tactic when breaking in horses. As the young horses whose eyes are bound beforehand, have never felt a saddle in their lives before, they do not even know what to expect and therefore remain completely stiff for the first moment. As soon as the rider is on the horse's back its eyes are unbound. It finds itself in an unbearable situation. In utter desperation it tries to shake off the weight from its back and bucks like mad. The rider, however, uses the whip on him so long until he runs away. This releases the tension and he runs until he is ready to drop. Surprisingly this is the moment at which most horses give up and subordinate themselves. Both come back fairly calmly after just 10-20 minutes. Sometimes the domador returns alone. From this point onwards the lessons successively until the horse becomes a real Criollo. At first glance this method seems very brutal, however the gauchos have their own opinion on the subject.

There is an enormous variety of colour amongst the Criollo breed. Many of these have been intentionally excluded from so-called civilised breeds. There are over seventy official coat colours and markings which are also entered in the stud book. It is a magnificent sight to meet a brightly mixed herd with different chestnuts, skewbalds, different greys and cremellos.

MARWARI HORSES

India's intrepid horses

Horses have been bred in Rajasthan for over 2000 years. The Chanan-Nomads wandered through the deserts and steppe areas of the Indian continent and created a very exceptional horse for their rulers which became renowned for its courage - and for its striking ears.

The Maharadscha's daughter watches the bustling activity in the inner courtyard from her window

We stand in the middle of a picturesque courtyard, the walls of which are decorated with stucco ornaments and colourful paintings. A huge wooden door, which closes the courtyard to the outside world, is covered in exquisite carvings. The courtyard belongs to »Rohet Garden«, a small summer residence of the local ruler's family, and this is where they breed their horses. Despite the early hour, the place is already a hive of activity: peasant women dressed in brightly coloured materials come past carrying water from the lake in large jugs, gracefully balanced on their heads. They giggle and laugh about the strange woman in her breeches and boots. The water buffalo is given a large pitchfork of fresh feed which is unloaded from a yoke of oxen. The Maharadscha's daughter watches from her window, keen to see what is going on. And in the centre of it all are our horses, all saddled up, held by men with impressive moustaches wearing large yellow and orange turbans. This world is fascinatingly different, – of a thousand different colours – exotic and irresistible.

In the next days and weeks my horse will accompany me through this foreign world, through clean little clay villages, through desert-like steppe areas and up into the Mewar mountain region with its cool forests and palaces standing in solitary splendour, like eagles' nests in the mountains. Slowly but surely it will convince me of its merits, and I will meet many people who will tell me more about this horse than I could read in any book. And after a while the special moment came which I had dreamed about before setting off on this journey: My fingers itch with curiosity. Very carefully I stretch out my hand and gently touch the delicate edge, stroke along the side and cautiously rub the sickle-shaped curve of the tip of the ear between my thumb and first finger. Finally I am convinced. This unique trademarkof the Marwari breed is not created by the human hand, rather it is a gift of God. I will still have opportunity enough to look at the different ear forms and the variations in ear length and curve, because these pairs of ears will be dancing around in front of my eyes for quite a long time.

Hardly any other horse breed in the world is so incorrectly judged, due to lack of information, as the Marwari horse. They are not merely the horses from India with the funny ears. The few really good Marwari horses which still exist are the tail end of a long traditional breed of highly qualified and perfectly trained war horses, which can be put on the same level as European breeds in the Middle Ages such as Lippizaners and Andalusians. The Haute Ecole of equestrianism with »Capriole« and »Courbette« was also taught in India, just with different names. 2500 years ago horses were already an important element of life in India. Bones of horses have been found which were given a ritual burial together with their master. Trade documents prove that horses were sold to the army of the Persian King Dareios when he went into battle against Alexander the Great in 333 B.C. Good horses were one of India's most important exports from antiquity until the beginning of the twentieth century. Special horses were decorated with jewels and fed with the juiciest dates from the princes' garden. The women of the ruling house visited the horses of their master and husband in order to anoint and bless them. Because they knew that the life of their loved one depended on the horse with whom he rode into battle.

The exceptional abilities of the noble animals, which were encouraged through breeding and training, were frequently praised in poetry and songs. The rulers of Rajasthan owned royal stables with thousands of horses. Reports about battles of the Mogul emperors in which the rulers of Rajasthan were involved, speak of 90,000 horses taking part. Mainly geldings or stallions were ridden, rarely mares. If you calculate how many mares and young animals are required in order to achieve 90,000 trained male animals, fit for battle, you end up with a total of 250,000 breeding animals. This means that horse breeding was one of the most important tasks in the realm. An entire army of grooms, trainers etc. was necessary in order to guarantee this organisation. In the archives of the Rajahs of Marwari some impressive documents have been preserved. In order to maintain the resilience and hardiness of the breed, the rulers gave the young animals into the hands of nomadic tribes who wandered through the stony deserts and steppe regions of Rajasthan. There they grew up and learned to cover long distances and to nourish themselves. In this way they experienced a special form of attachment to human beings. This attachment remained even when, later on, they were one horse among many in the huge stables. In the great »Shalihotra« saga all details concerning the keeping of horses are very precisely documented, and also the origin of the different blood lines, particular positions of crowns of hair or features of markings and colour of the coat. Every detail had its meaning and, as in the case of the Arabian nomadic tribes, conclusions were already drawn at the birth of a foal about its strengths and its character. The defeat of the Indian princes in the 19th century and the take-over of power by the British crown meant the death sentence for thousands of horses. They were simply slaughtered by the British army as the horse was considered inferior to the English Thoroughbred. Indirectly, this was intended to damage the pride of the princes, because the British knew well that the horses touched the most sensitive part of their souls. As the horses imported from England just dropped like flies however, they were forced to resort to the Marwari horses.

India's subsequent independence from colonialism meant a further, very considerable, deterioration in Marwari breeding in India. Under the British, who were outstanding horsemen, the Marwari breed was still granted minimal rights to an existence. The new government of socialist provenance, however, saw the horses as a symbol of power of the old rulers, however, and tried to dilute the breed. In order to cover the requirement for work horses, horses were imported from Russia and Poland. In just fifty years what had been bred and build up over hundreds, even thousands of years, the ideal war horse, idolised and glorified in sagas and legends and with a firm place in the oldest known literature, the Veda, was almost completely extinguished.

Only a few of these wonderful horses remained in pure form. Some of the ruling families never separated themselves from their horses and kept the breed going on a small scale. Also small farmers and landowners carefully protected and looked after their horses and tried to keep them pure. We owe it to some special people such as »Maharaj Narendra Singh of Mewar« that the reputation of the Marwari horses is improving again in India as well as internationally. He founded the Chetak Horse Society of India and every year at the »Chetak Horse Fair« he collects the best horses in India for a competition.

The fascinating and equivocal impressions of India are as enchanting as the eyes of the children.

Rajasthan is one of the most gloriously colourful and unspoilt regions in India with an overwhelming fullness of colour and scent, flowers and animals. It is the legendary home of the Rajputs, a powerful warrior caste who ruled the country for many centuries and possessed a very special war weapon, the Marwari horse. The breeding of the horses was subject to very strict laws embedded in the Hindu faith. The horses were considered to be a gift from the gods and as such were decorated with diamonds and gold. .

Every Marwari horse has them to a greater or lesser extent and there is no human influence on the growth. Horses of all colours have them and their fascination never wanes. It is believed that the Marwari horses originate from the Turkoman breed and, as a result of selective and intensive breeding by the Indian princes, they were developed into a unique noble breed which compares well with the European horse of the 18th century.

A brave war horse was the pride of every ruler. These rulers were excellent riders and believed themselves to be in complete unity with their horse, forming an inseparable bond in life as in death. This also explains the name of the horses, because Marwari means: »from the country of death«.

The stallion Ali Baba is the most famous dancing horse in the whole of India. He is an impressive, well-built black stallion with a white blaze who radiates incredible vitality. It's rare to experience a horse conveying such an intense sensation of innate musicality and pleasure in dancing. Together with his equally famous rider, Jodh Singh Rao, he achieves perfect harmony between human being, animal and music – a combination which in this style is unique in the world.

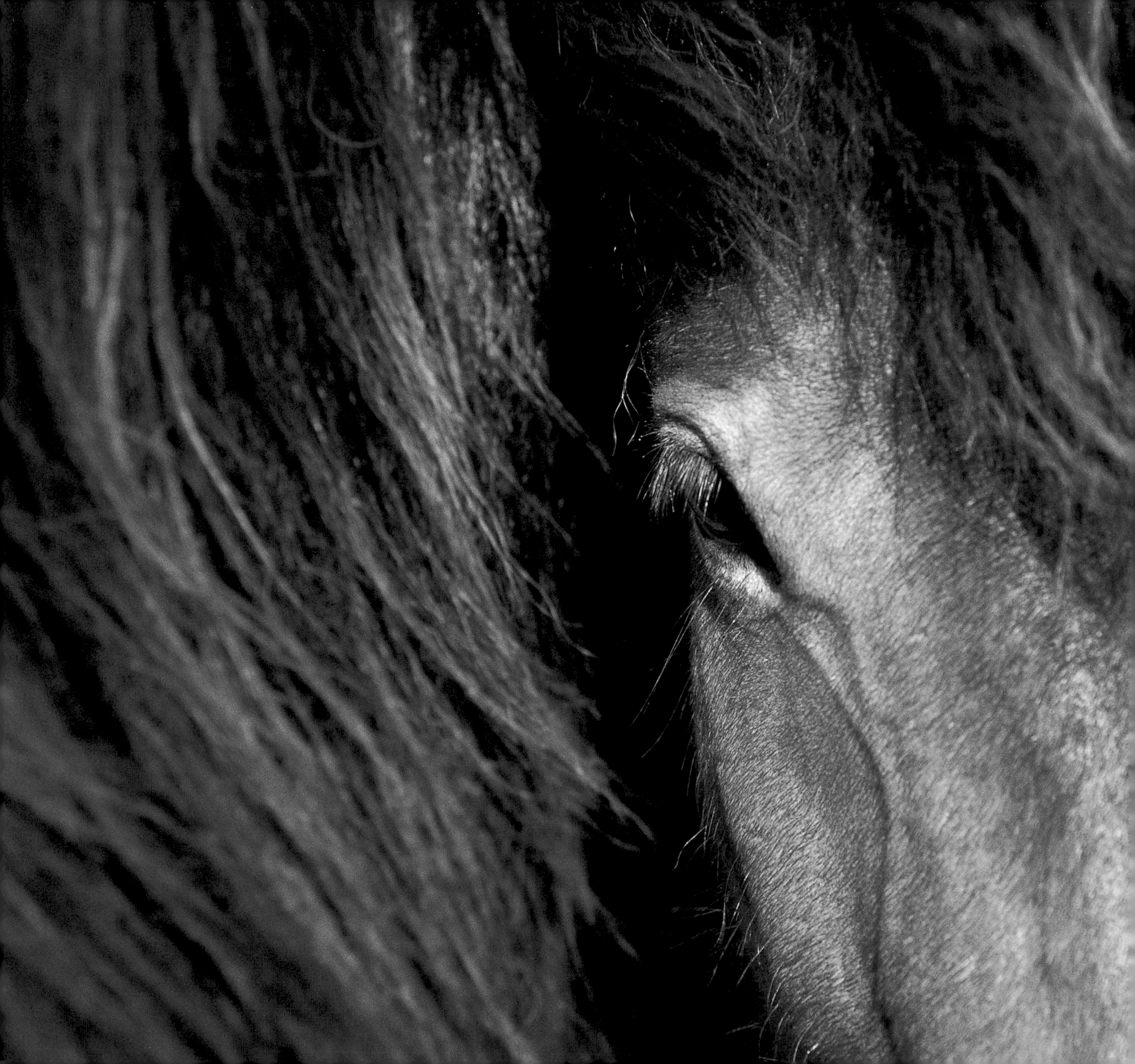

ISLANDIC HORSES

Viking horses from the volcanic island

In the golden light of the midnight sun, the Icelandic horses gallop across the unspoilt landscape with its glaciers and geysers. They have lived here, on the edge of the polar circle, for over a thousand years.

There they are – the famous Icelandic horses: a whole herd of small, shaggy animals – all of them an indefinable brownish colour, their coats caked with mud, their hindquarters turned defiantly into the strong wind. Here and there you can perceive a lighter patch of dirt – possibly camouflaging a grey horse. The rain runs through their soaking, shaggy manes and hits the ground in small torrents before seeping away into the quagmire. These horses have such thick hair that even their eyes and ears are almost completely concealed. They are standing in protective formation with all their heads facing inwards in an attempt to shelter from the cutting wind. Of course people had warned me about travelling here to the far north, but this far exceeded anything I could possibly have imagined... Typical Iceland! Driving rain, whistling winds, huge, wild clumps of cloud. And under these conditions I was supposed to spend two weeks riding and camping out.

The inhabitants of Iceland place a lot of importance on tradition and still worn on special occasions the historic old costume with the black cap and long tassle.

The worst, however, was yet to come – although on this first day I couldn't even have dreamt of it. The forces of nature were clearly against us. We rode through icy rain, and wild storms. One week later the weather got so hot that the horses' fair skin under their blazes burnt and peeled. We rode in the midnight sun to avoid sunstroke, and wore cloths over our faces as protection against the dust. These various trials and tribulations would have been bearable perhaps, but something else was to take me completely by surprise: instead of all these difficulties making me long to leave, I found myself becoming deeply attached to this country, these people, the completely mad weather and, above all, the four-legged inhabitants of Iceland. These small horses, who at first glance seem so very ordinary, soon transpired to be quite fantastic companions, like my black *Thor* who probably saved my life. Whilst we were trying to catch some young animals, a huge clod of earth came loose and slipped down into the river, carrying us both with it... We were immediately caught up in the pull of the strong current. The small stallion, to whom I clung instinctively in my state of shock, paddled with all the strength he had in him to bring us back to the bank. Had it not been for him, I would have had no hope of surviving in the ice-cold glacial water. *Thor* brought me across lava fields and through marshy fluvial plains where he was sometimes up to his stomach in mire. Iceland is as unpredictable as it is overwhelming. The only way to experience Iceland properly is on horseback. You don't get far on foot, and tracks up into the mountains are only passable for some months of the year with high-wheeled off-road vehicles.

Horses are the key to this country. When the Norwegian Vikings first settled on this still lonely volcanic island between 860 and 935 they brought sheep, cattle – and also horses – with them in their long open boots. They brought ponies of Celtic origin back with them from their crusades to England and Ireland and crossed them with their horses. This created the basis for later breeding of the Icelandic horse. As early as the year 1000 further importing of horses was forbidden for fear of epidemics. At the same time this ensured the genetically pure breeding of the Icelandic horse which has lasted for centuries and still creates great enthusiasm amongst equestrian experts today. It has also given the horses their name »Thoroughbreds of the North«. For their further development the Icelandic horses had to adapt to the extreme environmental conditions. Only those who could manage with very little nourishment under the most difficult of climatic conditions could survive. The natural selection – only the hardiest and most resistant could cope – ensured a robust constitution. This genetic inheritance is still firmly embedded in every Icelandic horse today.

For Vikings the horse was a sacred animal. Their highest god, Odin, undertook the wildest of adventures with his eight-legged horse Sleipnir. Amulets with representations of Sleipnir were considered to be good luck charms and promised strength and fertility. Horses also play a distinguished role in many other Nordic sagas and legends. They were the pride and wealth of heir owners. Special stallions made their masters famous and founded new breeding lines. They were also indispensable in coping with everyday tasks. Building materials were transported on horseback, post was distributed and every piece of material or item of crockery were fetched in this way. Even today Icelandic horses are used as pack and draught animals for all kinds of work on the island of lava fields, glaciers, stony deserts and rivers. And in this context these horses have another useful merit: an infallible sense of direction. Particularly in winter when snow drifts and thick mist make almost any other form of orientation impossible. It is quite possible that you are right beside your own front door and haven't realised it because of the dense mist. An Icelandic horse has an instinct which will bring him home over a distance of hundreds of miles, and he also senses every potential danger which may threaten.

Another speciality of the Icelandic horses is their natural ability to do five different paces. In addition to the walk, trot and canter, Icelandic horses can also do the old »pace«, (skeid) and »tolt«, which is called »rack« in the USA. The »pace« is done at running tempo over short stretches of a few hundred yards with the horse releasing tremendous power and energy. The »running pace« is described as a king's pace in Iceland. The »tolt« is in four-beat rhythm without a suspension phase so the horse alternatively has one or two hooves on the ground. The »tolt« can be ridden at working to running tempo and can actually reach a galloping speed. The horse has proud carriage and moves smoothly making it a comfortable gait to ride over long distances. The »tölt« is innate in Icelandic horses. At the end of the 19th century a start was made in the north of Iceland with selective breeding, paying particular attention to natural ability in the paces. In 1874 the first horse race took place in Akureyri in the north of Iceland. In many places today flat races at a gallop over different distances as well as pace races are held. Also popular are gait competitions. The largest Icelandic horse show is the »Landsmot«, a kind of national show at which the best breeding horses, super-tölters and running-pacers are presented. The first Landsmot took place in 1950 in Pingvellir, that historical place where 1000 years previously (930) the Althing, the oldest democratic parliament in the world, had first met. Since then the Landsmot has attracted many thousands of Icelandic horse fans. Their sure-footedness, their stamina, their strength and their calm temperament absolutely predestine them for leisure riding and trekking. Most impressive is always, however, to ride an Icelandic horse through the country of glaciers and geysers, lava fields and stony deserts – an experience during which any relation to space and time quickly becomes lost. It must have been the same in the days of the Vikings. The deep charm remains, today just as one thousand years ago – and anyone with any sense of life whatsoever will feel completely liberated and elated here.

Crossing rivers in the heart of Iceland is a risky undertaking because you never really know the strength of the current or the depth of the river.

This island on the polar circle, with its glaciers and geysers, is home to very special horses which grow up in unspoiled natural surroundings. They have an infallible nature and five different paces which make them one of the most comfortable horses in the world to ride. Today approximately 500,000 horses live in Iceland together with a population of 250,000 two-legged Icelanders.

Breeders of Icelandic horses are particularly proud of their wide variety of colours. A total of 15 different colours and colour combinations are recognised. Chest-dun and skewbald are the most common. A particular speciality are the so-called colour-changers - horses which are one colour in summer and another in winter.

Icelandic horses do not grow bigger than 13.00 to 14.00 h.h. Nevertheless they are considered to be horses rather than ponies. The foals have a very promising future ahead of them because Icelandic horses have a constantly increasing circle of supporters at international level.

An indescribable wind races through their magnificent manes and plays with them. Sometimes rain clouds make this volcanic landscape appear dull and dismal. Sometimes sunrays transform the misty plain into a magnificently illuminated landscape: a paradise with horses — a paradise for horses.

In the middle of the glacial area of the Myrdalsjökull a herd of horses is moving in the direction of Landmanna-laugar. Strangely shaped pillars of solid lava form the picturesque background, black volcanic sand the under-ground. The midnight sun enshrouds the entire scenery in breathtakingly beautiful light.

In front of the glaciers of the Vatnajökull, a volcano which is still active, a herd is moving in the direction of Hella. They are coming from the plateaux and now, in autumn, are going back home to the farmyard where they belong.

In Iceland lots of horses are kept semi-wild in herds. They spend the summer alone up on the plateaux. There they also give birth to their foals. In autumn they return to the lowland plains where, however, they still remain out in the open. Very social behaviour within the herd means that the young animals are protected against the extreme cold.

MAREMMANO

Semi-wild horses of Tuscany

In the »Maremma«, the marshes near Grosseto, semi-wild horses are still to be found. The north west of Tuscany is the home of the large brown »Maremmani«, which are considered to be one of Italy's oldest horse breeds. Together with the Italian cowboys, the butteri, they look after the long-horned cattle.

It's very early in the morning, shortly before sunrise and the damp coolness of the night still lies in the air. Davide shivers, pulls his coat more tightly around his shoulders, draws once more on his cigarette, so long and hard that the ash gives off a red glow, then he swings himself up into the saddle and sets off. His destination is the homeland of the brown Maremmano horses – an open area of land where the river flows out into the sea and the soft, alluvial ground smells of salt. The horses live there in the greatest freedom which mankind can possibly offer them. And Davide comes here because he is a »buttero«, an Italian cowboy. Every few days he checks up on the herd of mares down at the sea. Today I have arrived here first so I wait for him near the horses. As I approach one of the mares, who seems strangely excited and is running about with her ears laid back aggressively, I instinctively know that something is wrong. There is still no sign of Davide so I go a little closer and suddenly see foxes stalking through the grass. I notice that one fox is clutching something white as he runs off. The mare is still very worked up and keeps turning in circles, always moving around the same spot. Now, for the first time I catch sight of the newly born foal. It's still damp and its coat is sticky. But there are fresh bites in its ears and muzzle which are bleeding badly. The mare moved too far away from the herd, so the foal would have had no chance had I not arrived when I did. I sit down with the mare and foal and keep an eye on them until Davide finds us and can take care of the little creature. As the sun rises over the alluvial plain of the Ebro, we both wait patiently and watch the little creature when he manages to find his legs and do his first little bucks. Later Davide will put the mare and her foal into an enclosure where the injured foal can be looked after.

The young mare watches intently over her new born foal to ensure the foxes do not come too close.

The Maremma is a fascinating region in the south of Tuscany with dense pine forests, lonely beaches, marshy areas, thermal spas and nature conservation areas. Not far from Grosseto, in Alberese, an Italian state Stud still upholds the very old tradition of breeding an ancient type of tough, white long-horned cattle which are said to have been brought from Asia Minor by the Etruscans. This so-called Razza Maremmana is one of the last pure-bred cattle breeds in Europe and today they still live, as in previous times, in the »Parco Naturale della Maremma«, also known as the »Parco dell'Uccellina«, in an almost totally unspoiled natural setting. Here extensive grazing areas, uncultivated by farmers, are still to be found. The horse used for looking after these cattle is the robust Maremmano, which is also perfectly adapted to the marshy environment. It has grown up together with the cattle for centuries and therefore has developed a special instinct in dealing with them.

The Etruscans who settled in the area over 3000 years ago, thought highly of the small, tenacious horses and bred them as riding horses as well as draught horses for the two-wheeled »biga«. Their impressively decorated tombs bear witness to a distinctive cult of the dead which revolved around the horses. A black horse accompanied people during their terrestrial life and, once they entered the world of the gods, they rode a white horse. It is assumed that the early ancestors of the Maremanno horses are of Celtic origin, and the distinctive head shape seems to confirm this. In the year 225 A.D. a Celtic army, on its way to conquer Rome, advanced as far as the area of Talamone. There the 5000 soldiers were ambushed by the Romans and devastatingly crushed. Thousands of horses strayed across the countryside, some survived in the marshes and in time developed an amazing resistance against all kinds of diseases. This is why the Maremmano is one of the few animals in Europe which cannot get piroplasmosis, the disease passed on by ticks, which quite often ends in death. In the following centuries the wild horses were caught and crossed with horses of Spanish or Arab blood lines to make them more noble. The influence of the baroque Neapolitan horse is also documented. On repeated occasions they were crossed back again with the semi-wild horses, however, in order to keep the natural instincts and resistance in the breed. At some stage in the 19th century strong »Norfolk Roadsters« are said to have been imported from England and crossed with the breed. Today the Maremmano horses are well-known for their stamina, versatility, well-balanced nature and friendliness towards people.

Whatever blood flows in the veins of the Maremmano horses, the greatest challenge was and still is adapting them to the ruthless climate of their habitat: merciless sun in summer, stifling heat, hosts of pests which sting, bite and suck blood. Raw, damp cold in winter and a biting wind which covers absolutely everything with a thin layer of ice. Months of rain softens the ground and turns the alluvial land into a marsh so that the herds often stand knee-deep in the salty water. In summer, when the earth dries out and the grass shrivels up, the horses feed on thistles and a plant called salicornia, which is able to store salty water. They have relatively large hooves with a very firm layer of horn and also a constitution of iron because they never even see a stable until they are broken in. This is not done until they are three to four years old. The training method of the butteri is almost the same as the methods used by the gauchos in Argentina or the gardians in the Camargue. For the so-called doma, the breaking in, the butteri work in a corral, an enclosure which is similar to the »roundpen« used for Western horses. Two different saddles are used on the Maremmano: the »scafarda«, a modified eventing saddle built on a wooden tree, and the somewhat simpler but equally comfortable »bardella«. The Maremmano is a versatile horse which can be used in a wide variety of different ways. It has served honourably in the Italian cavalry and is still used today by the Carabinieri, the Italian mounted police. In recent years Thoroughbred blood has been introduced into the breed in order to produce a more true-to-type horse which no longer has a strong convex profile and is used intensively in sport. Today attempts are being made to latch on to the successes of the famous stallion *Ursus del Lasco* who achieved such outstanding results as a show jumper under Graziano Mancinelli in the 1970s.

Since Tuscany has discovered holidays on horseback and Maremmano horses and »butteri« came as representatives of their region to Equitana in Essen, Germany, the previously almost unknown Italian »cowboy« horse has come very much into the limelight. This, however, does not concern the Maremmano horses in the natural park in the slightest. When I return to them in the evening, a summer storm is brewing on the horizon, flashes of sheet lightening illuminate the dusky landscape very briefly. With his head held high and his mane flying, a powerful brown stallion trots towards me. He is completely caked in mud. His herd of mares and foals follows him closely. They gallop through the knee-deep water which floods the fluvial plain. They are free, in accord with the forces of nature, living in their own natural harmony which, thank goodness, has not yet been manipulated to suit the rules of human civilisation.

Davide is a buttero, an Italian cowboy. He spends a lot of time in the saddle.

One stallion lives together with approx. 10 to 15 mares in a small herd for half a year. The foals are born during this time. They are born without any human assistance and are immediately exposed to all the dangers associated with their wild state. The mares watch attentively over the new-born foals and the stallion also defends his offspring. Nevertheless almost a quarter of the foals die on account of the harsh climate or natural enemies.

The resistance and hardiness of the semi-wild horses from the Tuscan marshes have developed over centuries of surviving under the most difficult of circumstances. Increased efforts have been made with the breeding in recent years. The Butteri have always been considered indispensable in the breeding of Maremmano horses and cattle. Today they still embody typical traditions of the region and are regarded as an important symbol of the entire Maremma. For this purpose the »Associazione Butteri d'alta Maremma« has been set up in order to keep alive the original work and way of life of the Italian cowboys by means of public shows and presentations.

Maremmano horses are broken in according to a carefully structured sequence of progression. first of all the horse is brought into the corral where it becomes accustomed to lunging, i.e. it learns to respond to the voice and body movements of the human being. After several rounds of bucking and leaping about the horse accepts the leadership. The next day the lesson is repeated and then the saddle is put on before more lunging takes place. To prevent the horse from fighting too much against the saddle a second horse is brought into the pen and the new horse simply goes along with him. It is not until this stage that the buttero actually gets into the saddle, usually without any problems. Despite their long years of freedom, Maremmano horses are very kind, clever and cautious.

There's nothing more pleasant for foals than to grow up in a large herd. This feeling of security and belonging helps to develop a calm and well-balanced temperament. The fully grown animals are extremely robust. They normally stand at a height of over 16 h.h. Their typical colour is dark bay to almost black and they are very reliable and sure-footed, even in difficult terrain.

Page 224/225
The Alberese State Stud is located in the midst of open, flat countryside, extending into magnificent pine forests. In the distance you can imagine the glittering lights of the sea and the salty air can be smelt as far as Alberese.

The buttero always puts on a rough rope halter underneath the bridle. This means when he has other work to do, he always has the possibility of taking the bit out of the horse's mouth and tying the horse up with a rope.

Indispensable and, so to speak, a symbol of recognition, is the small stick called »uncino« with a hook at the end. It is a very important utensil for opening up wire catches on fences or simply lifting up little things without having to get out of the saddle.

The butteri ride in a very old version of a special saddle called a »scafarda« which has a very deep and comfortable seat for their long working days in the saddle. It also has various rings to which a lasso and other equipment can be attached.

The south of Tuscany is the legendary land of the Etruscans. It is here that they established some of their settlements and tried to dry out and cultivate the marshy area. The white cattle, the so-called razza maremmana, with their impressive horns have been at home here since Etruscan times. Horses in particular formed an important part of Etruscan culture and much evidence of this still remains today. Small bronze horses, for example, were popular burial objects. In the Palazzo Vitelleschi in Tarquinia, the oldest Etruscan town, it is still possible today to admire two magnificent terracotta horses dating back to the 4th or 3rd century B.C. They were discovered in an ancient settlement nearby in 1938. They had been in a prominent position, near steps which used to lead to a temple. Particularly striking are their powerful feathered wings.

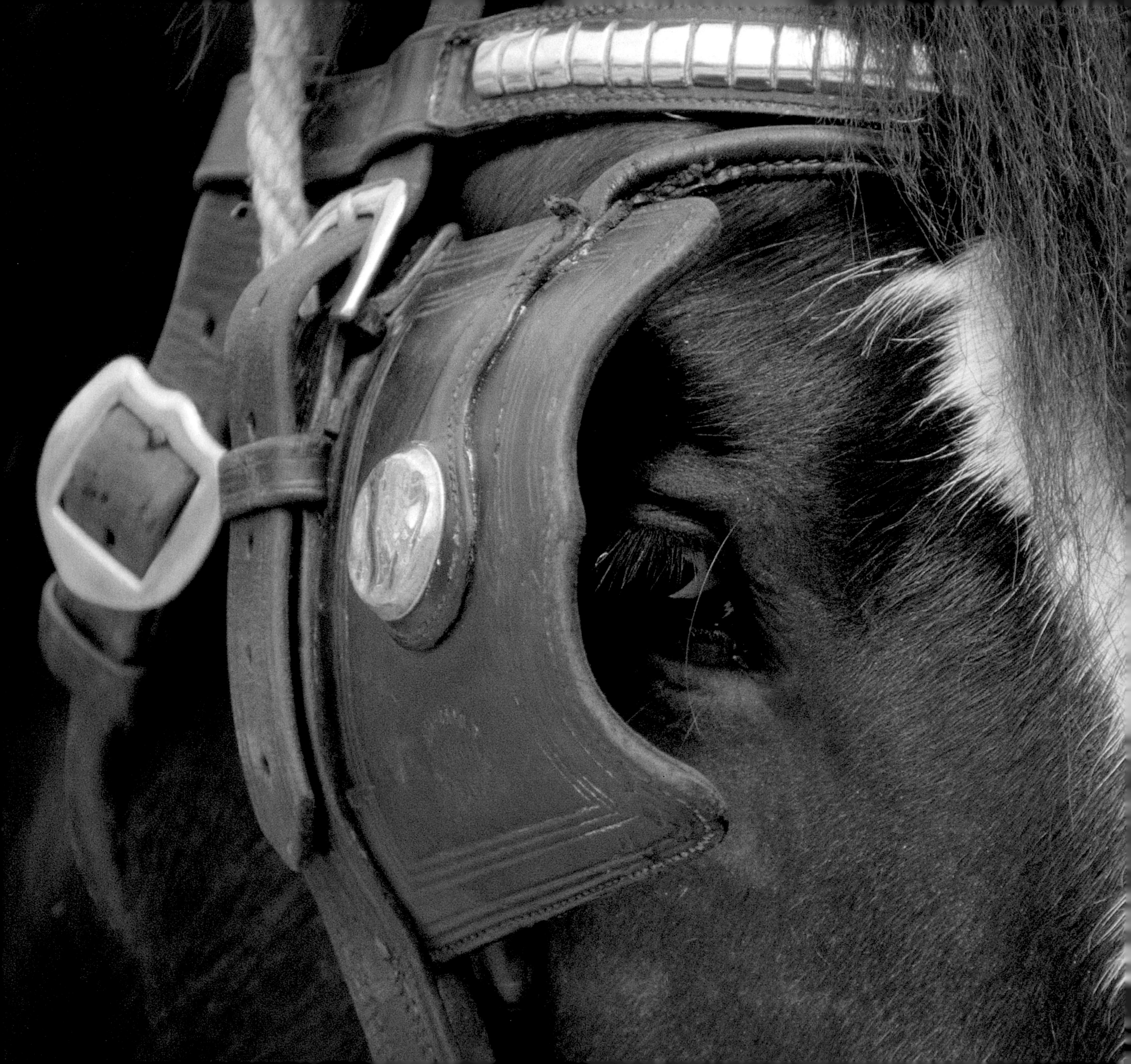

DRAUGHT HORSES

Powerful horses - loveable giants

For a long time draught horses in Europe were threatened with extinction. Just in time people remembered about their goodness and the services they had rendered. Today, throughout Europe, these gentle giants are once again being bred with loving care and are presented with pride on many festive occasions.

No fear of large animals: Shire Horses with their characteristic feathers hanging down over their fetlocks are considered to be extremely good-natured horses.

My grandfather was always very attached to his two chestnut Holstein mares who were kept in our stables. The large, hairy legs of these »field workers« were among the first objects to make a lasting impression on me in early childhood. When Fritz, my grandfather's old stableboy, got up on the box, he took the reins in his hand, clicked loudly with his tongue and the two draught horses pulled forwards. Then the rubber-coated wheels squeaked and the two horses braced themselves in their collar, willing to pull the load. I used to squeak with pleasure whenever Fritz lifted me up onto either *Lisa* or *Marie*. I clutched the thick mane with my small hands and felt quite out of this world. My grandfather worked his fields with these two chestnut horses, heavy work in the very fertile loam soil. He brought in the harvest with these horses. The two Trakehner stallions who were kept in the same stables were, however, only used as carriage horses.

Each country, each region, each different culture has bred its own working horse over the centuries. Each different type of soil, whether heavy or light, each type of work, whether ploughing or bringing in wood in winter, required horses which could adapt exactly to these conditions and at the same time be undemanding in their feeding requirements. From the huge Shires in England to the powerful mountain ponies of the Alps, the Haflinger was the most faithful working comrade, the farmer's true friend. They were often very close companions who understood each other without words and often had to face the cruel vagaries of the climate together. Hard physical work united man and horse. When, in the evening, the farmer gave his »workmate« one or two scoops of oats in the manger and then added a couple of carrots, this was always associated with a silent thank you and an affectionate slap on the hindquarters. Not until after feeding his horse did the farmer take off his dirty boots and go into the warm kitchen where his meal was waiting for him on the stove.

As a result of the mechanisation of agriculture and technical innovations in transport and traffic before and after the Second World War, draught horses gradually disappeared from the farms and were only seen very infrequently on the roads. Machines took over from animals. And this meant the end of a development extending back to the earliest times of human history. For centuries horses had been the only source of extra strength available to mankind to move goods and cover distances. Initially the horse carried loads on its back, for instance slaughtered game. Then the loads were put onto poles on the ground which the horses pulled behind them, until the introduction of the yoke in the Bronze Age, approx. 5000 years B.C. With the invention of the wheel the cart was developed and then the carriage. From this time onwards, the heavy horse was man's most important partner for doings and dealings, for transport and travel. After the Second World War warmblood horses were further improved with a view to high-performance careers in sport. The work horse as such had become superfluous and seemed threatened by extinction. Thirty years later, however, a revival of past values began: not just in the leisure area, particularly driving. These heavy horses were also rediscovered for doing environmentally friendly work, e.g. in the forest. At the same time there is renewed interest in the rich variety and history of individual draught horse breeds.

The North European Forest Horse appears to be the early ancestor of most breeds, including the »English Shire Horse«. It is said that the »Shire Horse« is descended directly from the »Great Horse«, that heavy Mediaeval competition horse which was found particularly in Northern Europe. Belgian Heavy Draught and Flemish stallions were crossed with knight's horses, particularly renowned for their strength and stamina, to produce England's heaviest and most popular work horse. Harnessed to a cart it can easily pull up to five times its own body weight. In the 17th century it was used to dry out the old marshlands in the English Fens and was subsequently bred there. The first stallion mentioned by name was called »Packington Blind Horse« and is said to have served mares in Packington between 1755 and 1770. Shire Horses are usually black in colour but there are also browns and even greys. Of course all Shires have the white hairs on their legs know as »feathers«, which completely cover their hooves. All horses are extremely large, standing at up to 22 h.h. and weighing approximately 1,300 kg. Their most outstanding feature, however, is their good-natured temperament and willingness to work.

The most widespread breed of draught horses in the 19th century – from a numerical point of view – were the Percherons. The real heavy weights amongst draught horses come from Normandy, from the Perch area to be more precise. It is also said, »the Percheron is an Arab, which, as a result of climate and the heavy work he has been doing for centuries, has become heavy«. Indeed the grey colour – which is also prevalent amongst Arabs – is found frequently amongst the Percherons, they also have very attractive heads and are very co-operative, willing and occasionally very lively. It is said that Karl Martell's Franconian army of knights were riding Percherons when they defeated the Turks at the battle of Poitiers in 732. By inter-breeding with Oriental horses, the very heavy draught horse was refined somewhat into a more pleasant riding and working horse with a long shoulder and ground-covering walk. And the Percherons also have their founding stallion. He was called *Jean le Blanc* and was born in »Mauves-Sur-Huisne« in Normandy in 1830. The French Stud Book was set up in 1833; since 1911 it has only been possible for an animal to be entered if both parents are registered.

The history of the Noriker breed extends even further back. 2000 years ago the former legionary horse of the Romans became established in the provinces of Noricum, Rhaetia and Pannonia. The breed only remained permanently, however, in Noricum. In the 16th century it was improved by the addition of Andalusian and Neapolitan blood. Norikers are still bred today in the Alpine region and in Southern Germany where very strict selection apply. Usually we see brown horses with light-coloured manes and tails, nevertheless the spotted horses or Pinzgauer are also popular. In all rural areas of Austria the winter time is used to drive out in horse-drawn sleighs. The farmers from the Goldegger Valley meet on the frozen lake. The freshly fallen snow crunches under the runners of the sleighs. At a temperature of minus 20° there is great laughing, mulled wine does the warming from the inside and a traditional felt coat from the outside. The horses are turned out in their Sunday best. Beautifully embellished leather decorations with brass fittings on which the name of the proud owner is engraved adorn the powerful horses' flanks. The same degree of care which is practised in the preparation of horses for representation purposes also applies in the breeding context. The selection criteria are strict. Today the Noriker has the largest self-contained breeding area of all European draught horse breeds.

Percherons, with their enormous tractive power, are regarded as ideal driving horses. This is why they are often used to draw large, prestigious carriages.

For centuries the chestnut Black Forest Horses with their light-coloured manes and tails have been bred in the isolated valleys of the area. These horses are always to be seen in the Black Forest at traditional processions or on festive occasions. The farmers used them to cultivate their fields, in summer they brought in the hay and in autumn the wood. In winter the horses were harnessed to sleighs. They also helped to bring the hand-made cuckoo clocks down into the valleys. Today the main breeding centre for these horses is the State Stud of Marbach. Little chestnut Black Forest foals romp around amidst the stud's own herds of Arabs and warm-blood foals.

On account of their kind temperament the Shire Horses in England are often referred to as »Gentle Giants«.

The powerful Shires, standing at a height of approx. 17.00 to 20.00 h.h. are the largest horses in the world. Their coat is dark brown to black and they have the well-known white »feathers« (long hair) on their legs. Very occasionally you also come across a grey. The tail is no longer docked but cut off short and decorated with woven straw or coloured ribbons on special occasions.

Today the Shire Horse is bred throughout England and Wales. The revival of the breed following decades of seriously diminishing stocks is, to a large extent, thanks to the breweries: some of them still uphold the tradition of using Shires to deliver their beer barrels to individual pubs. High-wheeled carts are used for this purpose and the horses wear an extra strong harness with brass decorations. Today Shire Horses are held in particularly high esteem by leisure drivers all over the world. At annual Shire Horses events the horses continually set new records with their impressive strength.

There is a saying according to which the Comtois was already bred in the Kingdom of Franconia. At any rate, it can definitely be traced back to the horses brought to Burgundy by the Teutons. The real breeding area is near the French-Swiss border in the »Franche Comté« - hence the name. A Comtois is a lively, cheerful horse as the stallion Aigle d'Or from the Pompadour State Stud in France impressively demonstrates.

The Comtois is related to the Ardennes Draught Horse, although it is of slightly more noble blood. In mediaeval times it served as a war horse and was also used as a cavalry horse in the 19th and 20th centuries. Nowadays Comtois Horses are used for light traction work, sometimes also in the Burgundian vineyards.

There is a unique atmosphere at the traditional Noriker Winter Meeting in Goldegg, Austria. The fresh snow crunches under the runners of the sleighs, the horses' bodies steam from their efforts - at an icy temperature of minus 20° centigrade.

Gabriele Boiselle… No life without horses!

The smell of hay and warm horses' bodies surrounds me. I am sitting amidst my horses and watching how they pluck some straw from the bale on which I am sitting. Every now and again a soft horse's nose runs over my toe and a rough tongue licks the sole of my foot. An odd satisfied snort interrupts the peace from time to time. The shadows of birch leaves dance on the horse's coats. The trees rustle and the horses' manes fly about in the spring wind. The single hairs of the manes look like spun silver draped around the horses' ears on which the sunrays cast a shimmering light. The origin of my work is here with my horses. Without my profound love of horses – my own as well as the many other – all other professional elements and even the best camera technology would be of no use. With my horses I re-establish harmony with myself and with the world. In this process I am nevertheless aware of the fact that horses are indeed animals, even though they are animals of a special kind capable of transposing a human being into paradise. In order to handle them properly you have to act firmly and exercise authority. If you are going to get on well with horses, you also have to get on well with yourself. Horses always have to feel clearly where they are with their people. Just as in a partnership with another human being, a successful partnership with a horse is based on the art of balance with the pivotal point being in the middle between unconditional love and a healthy awareness of oneself.

My horses always force me to take time: for them, for me and for what is really important – to sit here and watch them, *Faruk* for example, the twenty one year-old grey gelding. He was born here in my stable and was an obstinate horse right from the beginning – just like his mother. He always showed me what a bad rider I was – he threw me off dozens of times until he had taught me to stay on top and be the boss. With my horses I feel that they accept me as part of the herd. Willy, the black horse, drops some blades of hay into my hair and then fishes them out again. The hairs from his chin tickle my nose as he does this. Whenever I return from my travels, I always enjoy the sensation of being at home again and I really feel this most strongly when I go into the stable and hear the horses whinnying to me.

My soul is intricately linked to the horses. Stress and worries are quickly dispelled when I am together with my horses, or when my Trakehner stallion *Fritz* carries me far off and the pair of us enjoy a ride through the forest. Close proximity to my horses gives me inner peace and strength and is the source of my artistic creativity. Here I get the best ideas for my photos. When I observe the horses, study their movements, feel their behaviour towards the individual members of the herd, detect their respect or dominance on the basis of small gestures, then my mind becomes filled with images which I would like to photograph. I have learned only to take pictures which I really want to take, and only these ones are successful. Because they really tell what I think and feel – better than I could do myself.

G. Boiselle

It could be argued that Gabriele Boiselle has missed her true vocation... If she had been born a few thousand years earlier she would most certainly have fought alongside Penthesilea and her female warriors. Because just as these people were then, Gabriele Boiselle is a fighter, strong-willed and clever, courageous and unshakeable. And just as the female warriors before her, she also has a deep, natural love of horses, those noble creatures which play such an important role in her life and in her work. Unlike her ancient ancestors, however, the photographer does not nurture any belligerent ambitions – thank goodness! She has swapped the bow and arrow against a camera and fountain pen. And she uses these so powerfully that no-one can escape the fascination of her pictures and her texts. There is no question about it – Gabriele Boiselle is an absolutely top professional photojournalist. Sound training (journalism studies in Munich), first-class equipment and a comprehensive infrastructure (with her own publishing house) all go without saying. Far more important is the inner »professional« attitude, the far-sightedness with which, after some initial experience in the print, radio and television areas, she recognised photography as the most appropriate medium for her and horses as the subject which concerned her most deeply, thus dedicating herself to these two areas from this point onwards.

This was decision was taken over twenty years ago. Since then Gabriele Boiselle has travelled hundreds of thousands of kilometres – with her camera – has made the acquaintance of countless numbers of horses – and horsey people - and built up a photo archive, the quality and quantity of which puts it in a class of its very own. Each individual picture in the collection has its own story to tell, each story takes us – together with the photographer – on a special journey, in scorching sunshine and in the freezing cold, in the south of Africa or the fascinating Arabian world, in snowed covered mountain regions or stormy coastal areas. From A for Arab to W for Welsh Cob numerous horse breeds are represented in her archive. And she has dealt with each and every one of them in meticulous detail. In concrete terms this means that she has been to their places of origin, in the open landscape or in the homes of their breeders, she has followed their traces with her camera, regardless of the weather and often under extremely difficult conditions. The secret of her success is indeed to be found in this rare combination – on the one hand a highly sensitive aesthetic feeling for situations and special moments which should be captured by the camera, on the other hand an intrepid toughness not to be influenced by elementary adversities or indeed to be put off from any tasks she has set herself, and not least an infallible journalist sense to create something from this which becomes an unusual »story«, an exciting portrait, a fascinating (photo) report.

Gabriele Boiselle's photo art has meant that, for a long time now, she has been one of the most renowned equestrian photographers in the world. Her photos are published regularly in all important equestrian magazines, her calendars decorate thousands of walls every year and a very impressive number of copies of her books are published. But she is by no means at the finishing post yet. How could she be? As long as there are horses somewhere in the world whose tracks she has not yet followed, as long as there are equestrian photo stories to tell, and as long as there are people throughout the world to infect with love for these unique creatures – Gabriele Boiselle will continue with her work. How lucky for the horses – how lucky for us... As thanks to her pictures we are always able to keep discovering new aspects of the horsey world.

Rita Mielke

ANDALUSIAN HORSES

The Andalusian Horse is reputed to be descended from the Spanish Sorraia pony, which was possibly one of the first domesticated equine breeds in Europe. The »Pura Raza Espanola« (P.R.E.), as the Andalusian Horse is correctly known, owes its existence to the commitment of the Carthusian Monks of Jerez de la Frontera. In their monastery, founded in 1476, they made great efforts to establish pure breeding of the Andalusian blood line. At the end of the 14th century Spain had the largest cavalry in Europe and was able to boast possession of an excellent breed of horses. The quality of this breed was well-known far beyond the Iberian peninsular and indeed for 300 years Andalusian horses had a considerable influence on other horse breeds throughout Europe and America. The classical art of haute école, for which the Andalusian Horse was absolutely predestined with its agile, athletic build, was celebrated in the equestrian centres of all the royal courts in Europe. These horses are capable of tremendous collection and can therefore execute the classical figures of haute école to an inimitable degree of perfection. In the »Real Escuela Andaluza del Arte Ecuestre«, located in Jerez de la Frontera, presentations of classical equestrianism take place once a week. Meanwhile the Andalusian has also found its place in modern dressage sport, despite fierce competition from the German warmblood horses – as medals won at the Olympic Games and World Equestrian Games clearly prove. At the end of every year the ANCCE, the Spanish breeds society, holds a national competition in Seville at which a breathtakingly beautiful selection of the best horses in the country can be admired.

ARAB HORSES

Arab Horses, together with English Thoroughbreds, are the most widespread breed of horses. It is hard to find a breed anywhere which has not been refined by Arab blood at some stage. The occidental knights even returned from their crusades with Arab Horses. The blood of these animals was intended to make their own much heavier horses more hardy and agile as well as give them more stamina. Arab Horses seem to have a particular bond with human beings. Their natural affinity to human beings and the sensitivity with which they react to feelings and moods have given them the reputation of being a woman's horse. At the same time, it is also well-known for an Arab Horse to exceed its own physical limits in order to please its master or mistress. These horses combine an exceptional character with a lustrous appearance. Their fine skin and silky manes and tails are particularly striking, their lightness of movement and noble charisma beyond comparison. Different breeding directions exist under the general term of Arab Horse. Some are followed very successfully in Europe and the United States. Certain Arab fans prefer the pure »Asile Arab«, others are particularly fond of the light oriental type or the sporty strain with a good back and long neck. Common features include their height of just about 15 h.h. – although they are not ponies. In addition they have only 17 ribs and a pair of lumbar vertebrae and caudal vertebrae less than other horses. They can be used as sport and leisure horses as well as for driving.

BASUTO PONIES

The Basuto Pony is, so to speak, the national horse of Southern Africa. It is just as much at home in the mountains of Lesotho as in the woods of Zululand. It can draw a cart as well as it can serve as a reliable riding horse for tourists or as a work horse to look after the many herds of cattle belonging to the black clan chiefs. Since the 17th century it has developed into the most versatile horse in Southern Africa. Standing at between 12 and 13 hands, it has a frame which, although not particularly impressive at first glance, is capable of a incredible achievements. It has a long background history, however. European settlers brought the first English Throughbreds to the Cape of Good Hope as a method of transport for themselves as well as to be able to enjoy the pastime of horse-racing. Crossing with Barb blood and Spanish horses gave rise to an interesting new horse type known as the Cape or Boer Horse (after the Dutch settlers). Dutch and Portuguese trade ships also often brought small unpretentious Java or Zumba ponies from Asia and India with them to South Africa. The two breeds were crossed in order to combine the undemanding nature of the ponies with the better constitution of the large horses. The blessed breeders were the Basutos, a Bantu tribe which fought against the Zulus around 1870 and then had to flee to Lesotho with their horses. Humans and horses alike adapted to the extreme climatic conditions there and both have remained in the kingdom above the clouds ever since.

COMTOIS

The Comtois could be described as a horse of »powerful elegance«. It is related to the Ardennes Draught Horse, but is heavier than this breed. The horse has short, strong legs with broad joints but, despite its build, is of a fairly lively temperament. Above all, the Comtois is an extremely good worker, a characteristic which is especially appreciated when cultivating difficult vineyards or awkward woodland slopes. Comtois horses are particularly insensitive to heat and cold. This was of great benefit to Napoleon Bonaparte in his Russian campaign. He owed it to his horses that, despite the bitterly cold Russian winter, he was able to return to France with at least some of his army. Even in the Second World War Comtois Horses pulled French guns through the Ardennes and ensured ongoing supplies throughout the bitterly cold wartime winter. The Comtois Stud Book was set up in 1919 and the horses have been bred pure since 1925.

CRIOLLOS

The typical characteristics of a wild horse have been more strongly preserved in the Criollo than in any other horse breed. Thanks to the enormous expanse of the Argentinian Pampas, many Criollos still enjoy the privilege of growing up in freedom. The gauchos take great care to ensure that the horses have as little contact with humans as possible becasue they want to maintain the horses' instincts. In the first year of a foal's life it only comes near a human being once and has a halter put on its head. This act concludes its first lesson and subsequently it is left in peace for two or three years. A Criollo's stamina is proverbial. Its hooves are very hard, its tendons and entire locomotor system are completely indestructible. A Criollo can gallop for miles across the pampas. The horses are always kept in herds and never come into individual stables. After completing their work, they always return to the other horses. The breed was actually re-discovered by the Argentinian veterinary surgeon, Emilio Solanet. In 1911 he undertook his first expedition to Patagonia to try and find the legendary wild horses of the Indians. He drew up the first Stud Book and listed more than 70 colours. Particularly remarkable are the frequently occurring dorsal stripe and zebra markings on the legs. This indicates a direct connection to the still existing ancestor of the Iberian horse, the Sorraia pony. Anyone thinking about buying a Criollo horse should think about it very carefully however, because this robust horse is a very honest worker who doesn't really like idleness in European yards or solitary confinement in a stable.

FRIESIAN HORSES

The history of the Friesian Warmblood Horse can be traced back to prehistoric times. Back in the days of the Roman Empire Julius Caesar made use of the »equus robustus« which he had found in the Friesland region. Bones found show this ancient Friesian as being a light cold blood standing at 14 to 15 h.h. The development to a »Baroque horse« came about in the 16th and 17th centuries, when the Netherlands were occupied by the Spanish who brought their splendid Andalusian horses with them. The two breeds were crossed – and this was the beginning of the Friesian as we know it today. In the following 200 years the breeding of Friesian Horses absolutely flourished. They had a good command of the lessons of haute école, were reliable cavalry horses in the many wars which were inflicted upon the western world and they also paraded proudly in front of coaches and carriages. Then, however, the Friesian went out of fashion, mainly because strict breeding regulations prevented the breed being adapted to the taste of the times – a trend which almost made the seemingly old-fashioned Friesian extinct. It was only thanks to the great commitment of some Friesian farmers, who set up the »Het Friesche Paard« association in 1913, that we still have »the black pearls« today. Ironically it was precisely the strict pure breeding which almost became a disaster for the breed, which indeed preserved many of the much sought-after qualities which distinguish the Friesian as a leisure and family horse today. The most important of these is its kind, well-balanced temperament and its quickness and eagerness to learn – quite apart from its tremendous charisma and presence.

HAFLINGERS

The Haflinger today is a versatile leisure horse, approx. 14.2 to 15 h.h. which nevertheless still knows how to work hard. Its light-coloured mane and magnificent light tail are a special feature of the breed, often accompanied by light-coloured feathers on the legs. Its small, fine ears – which almost disappear under the thick mane – have been passed on by its Arab ancestors. The founder stallion of the breed is said to be »Folie 249«, son of a part-Oriental sire and an »Arab-refined« dam, who was born in South Tyrol in 1874. Haflingers are attentive horses and very willing to learn. They are of a very solid constitution, have enormous pulmonary volume and can live to an age of 40 years. Originally bred in South Tyrol near the village of Hafling, this charming mountain horse has long since conquered the whole world. There are active breeds societies throughout Europe, in North and South America, as well as in Australia and Asia. The Indian army has even used Haflingers in the Himalayas, in Kaschmir and Jammur. Their edelweiss brand with the H in the middle has become a symbol of their universal usefulness. From their beginnings as pack horses treading carefully along the narrow mule tracks in the Alps, they have now become very versatile leisure horses. Even in different disciplines of Western riding the Haflinger's powerful agility means it is able to compete successfully against Quarter Horses.

ISLANDIC HORSES

The Icelandic breed is unique because no alien blood has been added for over 1000 years. Icelandic Horses are robust and charming gait horses with very thick manes and tails and a height of 12.5 to 14.5 hands. Norwegian Vikings originally brought them to Iceland in the 9th century. The isolated location and the harsh climate favoured the development of the breed. Icelandic horses particularly distinguish themselves from other breeds by their five different paces – the pace and tolt – in addition to the »normal« walk, trot and canter. The famous tolt is special because it enables horse and rider to cover long distances comfortably within a relatively short time. Selective breeding of Icelandic Horses began in 1879 but it was not until relatively recently that their popularity became widespread and they began to take the European mainland by storm. Today more than 15 nations are represented in the International Federation of Icelandic Horse Societies. These horses' well-balanced temperament makes them very suitable for riding and driving, and much loved as a versatile family and leisure horse.

MAREMMANO

The exact ancestory of the Maremmani, the semi-wild horses from the Maremma in Tuscany, is somewhat blurred due to the many crossings which have taken place. Spanish and Barb blood is represented and also an Oriental element. In the 17th century powerful Norfolk Roadsters from England even became involved. More recently English Thoroughbred blood was added to improve the breed and to enable a further developement of the originally rustic horse into a sport horse. It has survived until today as a robust working horse of the Maremma cowboys, the butteri. The Maremmano is a very unpretentious, fairly large-boned horse which can grow to a height of 16 to17 hands. Its consistently dark brown, sometimes even black colour and the almost identical conformation of the horses indicates very consistent and homogeneous genetic make-up. It is important that, even today, the horses are still reared in a semi-wild state. Maremmano horses are completely reliable and therefore were also popular cavalry horses. The Italian »Carabinieri« also ride Maremmani.

MARWARI

The breed with the in-turned sickel-shaped ears is probably descended from the horses of Afghanistan or the horses of the nomadic tribes in Usbekistan and Turkmenistan. The traditional rulers of Marwar were outstanding riders and breeders, always looking out for the best equine material for their studs. On war raids into northern India during the 16th century they captured horses of the Turkoman type and brought them to the region known today as Rajasthan, where they were used to improve existing stocks. In order to maintain a broader basis for breeding they made their best sires available to their subjects free of charge and in this way improved the entire horse population of the realm. Under the Mogul ruler Akbar, the imperial cavalry is said to have owned tens of thousands of horses. The Marwari horse was an excellently trained war horse whose bravoury - according to historical documents - saved the lives of a considerable number of warriors. The lessons of the haute école, for example the »capriole« and »levade«, were taught here just as they were at the royal equestrian centres in Europe, and also for the same purpose. These special movements could catapult the rider out of the tumult of a battle and thus save his life. The decline of the Marwari breed began with the victory of England as a colonial power over the Indian rulers. Sadly only very few pure-bred horses remain today, nevertheless everything possible is being done to organise and save the breed.

MUSTANG

Mustangs are horses living wild in North America, descended from the animals which the Spanish conquerors brought with them into the New World. Spanish and Barb horses as well as cold-blood work horses have been crossed and given rise to a type of horse which, by means of natural selection in a harsh environment, has become the toughest horse of America. All today's Western horse breeds are based on Mustang blood, which was then improved by Thoroughbred imports from England and Europe. The name Mustang is probably derived from the Spanish word »mestena« which describes a group or herd of wild horses. Mustangs have a tremendous variety of coat colours and markings. Particularly popular are the »mouse dun«, the »buckskin« and of course all kinds of coloured horses known in the USA as »paints«. The mane, tail and legs are normally black. Mustangs grow to a maximum height of 14 to 14.2 hands and rarely have problems with their hooves or locomotor system. The horse is generally of a short build with low withers, sloping croup and a weight of approximately 350 kg. Just as an Arab, a real Mustang has only 17 ribs and 5 lumbar vertebrae instead of 6. In the 1960s the Mustang population was so drastically reduced that in 1970 legislation had to be passed to protect it as a species threatened by extinction. Today there are many organisations which take care of the stocks. In the mountains of Oregon or Nevada it is now occassionally possible once again to see wild herds roaming.

NORIKERS

Over half the horses in Austria and Switzerland are Norikers or are descended from them. This long-established and down-to-earth breed has constantly had to adapt to new living and working conditions. Despite this, it has always maintained its character and the fundamental features of the breed. The early Romans immediately appreciated these and encouraged breeding in the province of »Noricum«. Via the narrow mule tracks of the Alps, the Noriker soon spread as far afield as Italy and France. Breeding in the area of Austria was concentrated in Juvavum, located near present-day Salzburg. In the16th century the monasteries took over responsibility for horse breeding, established large studs and improved the typical features of the breed. Under the auspices of the Archbishop of Salzburg a breeding standard was specified for the first time and refinement with Spanish and Neapolitan blood lines was systematically practised. Today different strains of the Noriker are recognised, the Kaerntner, Steirer, Tyrolean and South German Cold-blood. Pure grey horses are rare, more common are dark dapple greys with a black head. Dark bays and different shades of chestnut are most frequent, often with light manes and tails. Today, as in former times, the spotted horses are considered very attractive and as such make up a special strain known as the Pinzgauer Noriker.

PERCHERONS

The origin of the Percherons extends back to the time when Karl Martell achieved victory over the Moors. The spoils of war also included horses which were then crossed with the local mares. At a later stage Arab horses also became involved: in 1099 Robert Graf von Rotrou brought a very special souvenir back with him on the occassion of his safe return from the first crusade to the Holy Land, a small collection of Arab horses. He used them to further improve the local draught horses. Louis XIV founded the »Le Pin« stud in Normandy, which is still one of the most important stallion stations for Percherons today. Two outstanding Arab crossings were the famous half bred stallions *Godolphin* und *Gallipoly*, sire of the most famous Percheron stallion *Jean le Blanc*. Standing at a height of 16.2 to 17 hands Percherons exude an air of powerful dominance, although they do not make an over-heavy impression. They have an attractive head with small ears, an inheritance from their Arabian ancestors, and are relatively agile despite their corpulence. Today the Percheron still remains a very versatile horse which adapts easily to changes in climatic zones and allocated tasks. In its long history it has served the human being as a war horse and carriage horse, as a draught horse working in the fields, also as an artillery horse and a riding horse. Between 1880 and 1920 the breed experienced a final zenith – thousands of animals were exported to the huge farms founded by European settlers in South America, Australia and South Africa. Prior to the First World War the number of animals entered in the Stud Book had risen to over 30,000.

BLACK FOREST HORSES

Typical for the Black Forest Draught Horse is the usually liver chestnut colour, and a contrastingly light-coloured man and tail. A Black Forest Horse is the pride and joy of its owner and today is used particularly for representation purposes, at traditional processions and festivities in the Black Forest. The breeding of a typically rustic horse which originated in medieval times was further developed by the addition of Pinzgauer, in other words, Noriker blood. In 1896 the Black Forest Horse Co-operative was founded, which subjected the horses to strict breeding criteria from then onwards. The aim was to develop a draught horse with a strong muscle structure which was not too heavy. Stallions from the Ardennes, from the Rhineland and from Unterbaden contributed to the success of breeding efforts on the medium term. Today the State Stud in Marbach takes on the Black Forest Horses. At a height of approximately 15 hands these chestnut horses are powerful as well as attractive – their coats often shine like brass in the sun. The population is growing and the breed is gaining new friends constantly.

SHIRE HORSES

Shire Horses, standing at a height of 17.2 to 21.2 hands, are considered to be the largest horses in the world. Their coat is dark brown to black and they are also well-known for their white feathers (long hairs) on their legs. Their tails are no longer docked but rather cut off at the end of the vertebral column and decorated with raffia or coloured ribbons on special occasions. Preparing a Shire Horse really well for a show takes many hours of work. The Shire breed has not always been so large. It is estimated that in the 16th century the »Great Horse«, an ancestor of today's Shire Horses, was just about 15.3 to 16 h.h. As a result of intensive breeding over centuries an extremely strong horse developed which was used for loading and unloading ships in the ports of Manchester and Glasgow, for example. Nowadays some breweries make use of the Shire Horse's popularity for adertising purposes. In Stratford-upon-Avon the »BRASSbrewery« has several teams of horses which deliver barrels of beer in traditional style on high-wheeled vehicles. It can frequently be observed how, after a day's work, the horses are given a whole bucket of beer by the coachman – which they consume with obvious pleasure.

QUARTER HORSE

The Quarter Horse is the most American of all horses. Millions of them are entered in the Quarter Horse Register, making it the largest breeds society in the world. If we add all the various crossings, we can say that some representatives are to be found on almost every ranch and on every yard in the United States. It is the perfect work horse for the cowboys, fast, unpretentious, eager and willing to learn and at the same time well able to fulfill the different expectations of leisure riders. On long-distance or endurance rides it shows enormous qualities. Breeders can now achieve good prices for these horses and some very successful sires cost a fortune. A Quarter Horse is normally bay or chestnut and stands at a height of 15 to 16 hands. It is a compact, very muscular horse. The genetic inheritance of this breed can already be seen in newborn foals: its wide chest, flat withers and broad back as well as the well-formed hindquarters are outstanding physical features of the breed. The muscles between the hindlegs show where this horse's »motor« is located. There are 12 big Quarter Horse lines, which can all be traced back to the two founding sires of the breed – *Janus* und *Sir Archy*. *Janus*, who died in 1780, was the more significant of the two and through his son *Printer* he founded the more important line. The lines of *The Shilo*, *Old Billy*, Steel Dust and *Cold Deck* can be traced back to *Sir Archy*. Pedigrees and bloodlines have a certain prayer book quality for genuine Quarter Horse fans – they are learned off by heart because specific qualities are passed down through these lines.

ACKNOWLEDGEMENTS

Unfortunately it is not possible to mention by name everyone who has helped me on my journeys, whose hospitality I have been able to enjoy, and without whose concrete support some trips would certainly have turned out rather differently. I should like to express my most sincere thanks to all these people. In particular, I should like to thank Bayard and Mel Fox, two good friends who have travelled with me and introduced me to special people and places. The same also applies with regard to Diethard Franz.

I owe a special thank you to my loyal team at Edition Boiselle, who have supported me for many years: Anette Harenburg, Ula Rafail, Marielle Andersson, Ingrid Wawrok, Siggi Maurer and Reinhard Harz. They all surround me with an atmosphere of friendship and warmth and motivate me in my work – even in the difficult times.

Finally, I should like to thank my mother for the support she has always given me – although there have been occasions when it was not possible for her to comprehend my actions.

I believe that special abilities and talents are not simply a matter of fate - rather they are a special gift. Therefore my very last words of thanks are addressed to the one who has endowed me richly with so many gifts.

This edition is published by Barnes & Noble, Inc.
By arrangement with Feierabend Verlag OHG

2004 Barnes & Noble

Project Coordination & Design: Petra Ahke
Graphic Director: Erill Vinzenz Fritz
Translation from German: Carol Hogg, Osnabrück

Production: Stefan Bramsiepe, Essen
Reproductions: farbo print + media GmbH, Cologne
Printing and Binding: Druckhaus Locher, Cologne

Printed in Germany
ISBN 0-7607-6215-5
61 90008-1